Albert Manke

Coping with Discrimination and Exclusion

Experiences of Free Chinese Migrants in the Americas in a Transregional and Diachronic Perspective

INTER-AMERICAN STUDIES
Cultures – Societies – History

ESTUDIOS INTERAMERICANOS
Culturas – Sociedades – Historia

Volume 32

Albert Manke

Coping with Discrimination and Exclusion

Experiences of Free Chinese Migrants in the Americas in a Transregional and Diachronic Perspective

Wissenschaftlicher Verlag Trier
Copublished by
UNO University of New Orleans Press

Coping with Discrimination and Exclusion:
Experiences of Free Chinese Migrants in the Americas in a Transregional and Diachronic Perspective /
Albert Manke. –
(Inter-American Studies | Estudios Interamericanos; 32)
Trier : WVT Wissenschaftlicher Verlag Trier, 2021
ISBN 978-3-86821-829-9
New Orleans, LA: University of New Orleans Press, 2021
ISBN 978-1-60801-207-7

SPONSORED BY THE
Federal Ministry of Education and Research

The project, on which this book is based, has been funded by the German Federal Ministry of Education and Research (Bundesministerium für Bildung und Forschung, BMBF). The responsibility for the content of this publication lies with the author.

Cover Image: "The Great Fear of the Period: That Uncle Sam may be swallowed by foreigners. The problem solved." San Francisco: White & Bauer [between 1860 and 1869]. Digital ID: pga 03047. http://hdl.loc.gov/loc.pnp/pga.03047 (accessed March 23, 2019). Courtesy of the Library of Congress Prints and Photographs Division, Washington, D.C., 20540 USA.

Cover Design: Brigitta Disseldorf

Library of Congress Cataloging-in-Publication Data
Names: Manke, Albert, author.
Title: Coping with discrimination and exclusion : experiences of free Chinese migrants in the Americas in a transregional and diachronic perspective / Albert Manke.
Other titles: Experiences of free Chinese migrants in the Americas in a transregional and diachronic perspective
Description: Trier : WVT Wissenschaftlicher Verlag Trier ; New Orleans : University of New Orleans Press, 2021. | Series: Inter-American studies; 32 | Includes bibliographical references.
Identifiers: LCCN 2020044527 | ISBN 9781608012077 (paperback)
Subjects: LCSH: Chinese--Foreign countries. | Asians--America--Social conditions. | Immigrants--America--Social conditions. | Transnationalism--Social aspects--America. | Racism--America. | Xenophobia--America. | Chinese diaspora.
Classification: LCC DS732 .M35 2021 | DDC 305.8951/07--dc23
LC record available at https://lccn.loc.gov/2020044527

Publisher: WVT Wissenschaftlicher Verlag Trier, Postfach 4005, D-54230 Trier, Bergstraße 27, D-54295 Trier, Tel. 0049 651 41503, Fax 41504, www.wvttrier.de, wvt@wvttrier.de

Copublisher: University of New Orleans Press, 2000 Lakeshore Drive, Earl K. Long Library, Room 221, New Orleans, LA 70148, United States, 504-280-7457, unopress.org

This publication is an outcome of the collaborative research project "The Americas as Space of Entanglement" at Bielefeld University. The author's research was generously funded by the German Historical Institute Washington and the Volkswagen Foundation as well as by the German Excellence Initiative through the University of Cologne and its Global South Studies Center. The author sincerely thanks Megan Hanson for her translation of this study from Spanish to English.

Contents

Introduction 1

1. Migration, Exclusion, and Strategies of Resistance 6

2. The Period of the Manila Galleon: Chinese and Spaniards in the Philippines 11
   2.1. The Philippines as an Axis of Global Trade and Space of Conflict, Sixteenth and Seventeenth Centuries 16
   2.2. Transpacific Asian Migration to Continental New Spain 25
   2.3. The Philippines of the Eighteenth Century: Consolidation, Miscegenation and the Regulation of Migration 27

3. Forced Migration and Voluntary Migration in the Modern Age 35
   3.1. From the Age of Revolution to the Great Migrations 35
   3.2. The Coolie Trade – an Intermediate Step toward Voluntary Labor? 38
   3.3. What is Free Migration? 46
   3.4. Asian Immigration as a Part of the Free Migration to the Americas 50

4. Free Migration of Chinese to the United States 53
   4.1. In Search of the Gold Mountain 53
   4.2. The First Phase of Discrimination of Chinese Immigrants (1848–c. 1865) 61
   4.3. Building the Transcontinental Railroad and a Time of Hope during the Reconstruction Era 77
   4.4. The 1870s: A Time of Change 87

5. Inter-American Entanglements: Spreading Xenophobia? 95
5.1. Transregional Exclusion: USA and Latin America 95
5.2. Transpacific Cooperation between Asia and Latin America and Resistance in the Late Nineteenth Century 101
5.3. Circular Migration and Transnational Networks 104
5.4. Hegemonic Power and the Proliferation of Policies of Exclusion in the Americas 105

Conclusions 115

Works Cited 121

When we were first favored with the invitations of your ship-captains to emigrate to California [...], we could hardly have calculated that we would now be the objects of your excessive hatred [...].

Every nation under heaven mocks at you. Hence it is not alone we Chinese that suffer, but blessings are lost thereby to your own land.
—Pun Chi in Speer (1870, 596, 602)

Introduction[1]

Xenophobia and racism are currently relevant and worrying, not only in the United States of America and Europe. This often manifests itself in hatred toward 'undesirable' immigrants. The public discourse of populists tends to justify this aversion by claiming that the migrants themselves are to be held responsible for this very aversion and not those who are aggressive toward and reject them. Prejudices based on supposed differences or cultural, ethnic or religious inferiority are the breeding ground for dynamics of discrimination and exclusion that not only infringe upon the human rights of immigrants, they are also harmful for the receiving societies and their economies. Repressive policies of 'zero tolerance' or a 'heavy hand' toward immigrants result in the criminalization of immigrants that by itself keeps fomenting the increase of xenophobia and racism.

1 This study is based on previously published literature and sources and shall provide a preliminary framework for my larger research project about Chinese migrant networks in the Americas during the Exclusion Era. Currently conducted at the University of California, Berkeley, this project will include new archival research on Chinese migration and the multiple ways of thinking the Americas otherwise through informal networks like Chinese secret societies.

During the Cold War there was a decrease in racist and xenophobic policies and practices in developed countries, both within societies as well as in the design of migration regimes. However, since the 1990s there has been a new rise of racist and xenophobic attitudes that are now coupled with populist policies of the right and far-right. These tendencies have a direct impact on the formulation of exclusive migration policies and the renovation and deepening of the pre-existing structures of xenophobic discrimination.

Attitudes like these have been fostered by the heyday of neoliberalism, growing inequality and economic crises, have led people to experience the contact with new generations of immigrants fleeing from unlivable conditions as culture shock, increasing estrangement between people.

Nowadays, more attention is being paid to the rise of xenophobia, racism, and populism while the cycle of discrimination of migrants is interwoven with the social question and the decline of living conditions in the countries of origins in the globalized world (Faist 2018; McLeman, Schade, and Faist 2016).[2] A number of ideas have emerged in order to counteract this disturbing situation and stop the cycle of xenophobic hatred, such as a global network to create an operative framework that helps formulate policies against xenophobia when developing migration policies (Achiume 2018).

While there are now international organizations such as the United Nations that have the power to raise awareness about these problems and exert a certain amount of pressure on government that do not follow through with their promises in this regard, these types of mechanisms had not yet been established in the nineteenth century. The mistreatment of immigrants posed more of a bilateral problem between two nation-states and only gained attention when incidents greatly affected international relations, especially commercial

2 Furthermore, there are three key aspects that contribute to the decline in living conditions and foment an aversion toward immigrants: economic inequality (in the societies of both the country of origin as well as the receiving country), climate change and armed conflict (or higher levels of violence).

ones. However, as Adam McKeown has shown for this time period, the implementation of policies that regulated populations and excluded migrants had implications on a global scale with respect to the development of border regimes. In his conclusion he emphasizes the continuities of the discourse surrounding immigration, inclusion, and exclusion from the nineteenth century to today:

> A sense of crisis pervades public discussions of migration, both now and for the past two centuries. There is seemingly no end to the [...] tales of migrant suffering, stories of migrant success and migrant dreams, econometric calculations, policy adjustments, strange coalitions, unintended consequences, incommensurable interpretations and uncompromising polemics that are the raw material of these discussions. This material is worked into endlessly contentious arguments about the virtues, vices, assimilability and contributions of immigrants, the scope and meaning of rights, the obligations of asylum, and the nature of national community. [...] From the perspective of two hundred years, however, the arguments about migration are numbingly familiar. [...]
>
> Some of the most notable (and potentially reversible) of these trends are the decline of caste, blood, race and discretionary dictation tests as legitimate modes of exclusion, the rise of remote control, and the continuing proliferation of occupation- and wealth-based preferences as favored categories of selectivity. Broadly, this can be seen as a shift from attributes to achievements as the basis of selection, the latter being a more acceptable mode of discrimination in a meritocratic world. (McKeown 2008, 349-350)

Published in 2008, the ideas he formulated in the last paragraph quoted here are already being questioned today by openly racist migration policies, which are being propagated by the current governments in the USA, Brazil and various European countries. According to these types of observations, one can draw a diachronic comparison between the problem of discrimination against immigrants today and nearly 200 years ago. It is therefore pertinent that this study revisits the first establishment of the control of voluntary migration and identifies the dynamics of the exclusion of immigrants.

Since they were the first to be affected, this study will use the Chinese as an example to reveal cycles of exclusion and xenophobia in the Americas and explain some of their coping strategies. It will point out the aggression and structural discrimination these immigrants were confronted with. Furthermore, this study will highlight some acts of resistance and empowerment that appear to be part of the structures of resilience that these groups have developed in the face of severe persecution and exclusion. This is a necessary and specific contribution that is linked to current studies on migration, racism, and exclusion in the Americas and elsewhere.

In showing that both, local action and transnational networks have played a role in the dynamics of resistance, this study will have a truly inter-American focus on processes of exclusion and (to a lesser extent) of resistance by highlighting the challenges that the Chinese communities have had to face in the Americas. The focus on this diaspora locates Chinese communities in various regions of the Americas where they create spaces that overlap, interact, and influence one another, which could contribute to a better understanding of the Americas as an interconnected and interwoven space.

To form the temporal framework of this study, we consider it pertinent to primarily compare two large cycles of voluntary migration of Chinese to the Americas and patterns of their exclusion: that which occurred to the Philippines (under Spanish colonial rule) during the early modern era (especially between 1571 and 1639), and that to the United States, Canada and various Latin American countries in the late modern era, especially between 1850 and 1943. We recognize the outstanding importance of forced migration and the multifarious abuse of slaves and other migrants who were coerced to migrate against their will. Even so, this study will not just analyze this well-studied topic; it will specifically examine the discriminatory dynamics that developed around voluntary migration of 'non-white' migrants and their encounters with migrants of European descent in the Americas. Before analyzing voluntary migration in the late modern era, however, this study will briefly outline the semi-voluntary migration of contracted workers from Asia, the so-called 'coolies,' during the nineteenth century. This periodization is supported by Eltis, according to whom over the course of two centuries (from 1630 to 1830) forced migration "was by far the most dominant regime under which population movements occurred" (2004, 314). It can therefore be deduced that before and after this period, the majority of migration in the Americas was voluntary. The following graph has been made on the basis of these observations.

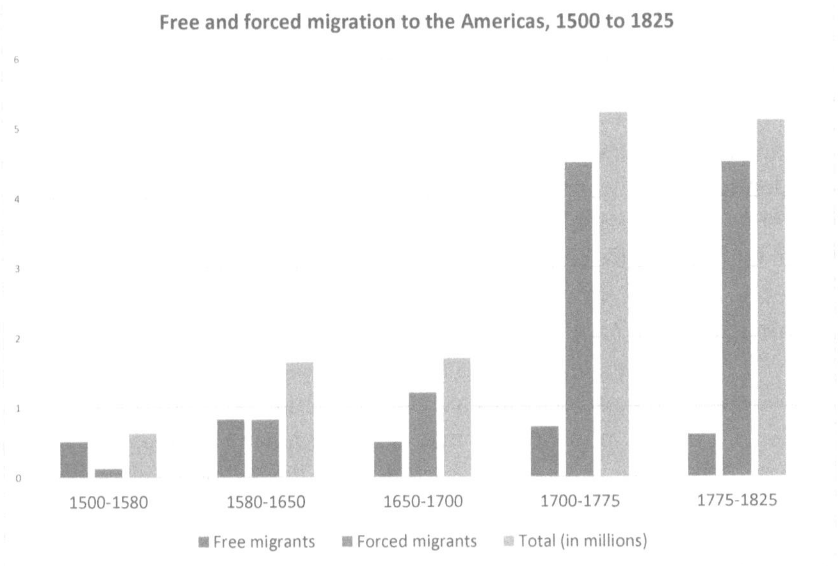

Table 1[3]

3 Approximation based on data from Lucassen and Lucassen (2009, 355, from the period 1500 to 1800), Zeuske (2013, 457), and Eltis (2004, 315). Eltis' categories "contracted" and "coerced" were compiled in the category "forced migrants." Voluntary migration from Asia was not included due to insufficient data; known numbers are in the few thousands.

1. Migration, Exclusion, and Strategies of Resistance

Since the beginning of European expansion in the Americas, Africa and Asia, European conquistadores and colonizers used methods of social, economic, and political control that resulted in discrimination, exclusion, and extermination. While in the Americas alliances were formed with indigenous peoples and large processes of miscegenation took place, social hierarchies were generally based on xenophobic and racist prejudices that in turn were based on ideas of ethnic and cultural superiority. This process facilitated the exploitation of indigenous populations and was reinforced and repeated by the trading of African slaves and slavery until its abolishment in the nineteenth century. With respect to the causes of forced migration in order to feed the extractivist system based on slavery, Rediker, Pybus, and Christopher stated that "[...] the rise of capitalism from the late sixteenth century onward forced millions of expropriated people to make middle passages from Europe and Africa to the Americas" (2007, 2).

With the rise of nation states, a two part mechanism began to develop in the new republics: on the one hand, there arose the objective of forming populations that were ethnically adapted to racist ideas of the European elites; on the other hand, they were working to create a 'nation' in which a growing part of the population was being granted civil and citizenship rights. This process of inclusion in the republic in the original sense of not only a 'public affair' but an 'affair of the people' (*res publica*) began with the bourgeois revolutions, wars of independence and the rise of liberalism that gradually provided access to political and economic power to groups that had previously been mere colonial subjects. The right of belonging to the budding nation and to participate in the political and public spheres were based on markers of ethnicity, language, nationality, gender, social status, age, and education level, among others.

The creation of the nation and the granting of access to it to certain groups of people at the same time meant denying others access to it. In some Latin American countries immigration was a decisive factor in the creation of the nation. However, in this process, during which new parts of society such as workers were being empowered, the perception of competition and hateful ideas started to crop up. Coupled with ideas of ethnic superiority that were fully established in a large part of society, the results were discrimination, exclusion, and persecution based on xenophobia, racial hatred and taking advantage of the lack of protection for the affected groups.

The first group of migrants to suffer the consequences of this process and these attitudes were Chinese immigrants. In the Spanish empire, not only indigenous populations, but also Chinese and other Asian groups that migrated there in search of economic opportunities had to face discriminatory and exclusive practices. During the era of the Manila Galleon, which linked the Philippines with the rest of the Spanish colonies for more than two centuries, the Chinese community in Manila had to suffer repeated, severe persecution. However, time and again this economically successful community recovered and developed strategies to overcome multiple forms of discrimination and exclusion. During the second half of the nineteenth century and the first decades of the twentieth century a similar process took place among voluntary Chinese migrants in the USA, Canada, and Mexico who were looking for a better life.

There were also cycles of exclusion and discrimination of Asians in other parts of the Americas, both within and outside the contract system of the coolies, a system of quasi-slavery. Two sadly culminating dynamics of exclusion were the Chinese Exclusion Act that was passed in 1882 by the federal government of the United States, and the anti-Chinese campaign in various states of northern Mexico that was started during the Mexican Revolution. In the United States, the anti-Chinese law not only rang in an era of exclusion for Asians that was to last until 1943, it also set the standards to control access of all immigrants against the background of a racist paradigm that remained officially in place until the Immigration and Nationality Act of 1965. Furthermore, this policy was exemplary for the development of migration regimes in various Latin American countries (especially in Argentina, Brazil, and Cuba), in Canada, and Australia, where settler colonialism and the White Australia policy were practiced.

This study takes an inter-American and transpacific look at historical processes of discrimination and exclusion of migrants in the Americas based on racist and xenophobic prejudices. It will focus on pertinent migration policies and conjunctures of negotiation in various societies of the Americas while highlighting discriminatory dynamics in their diachronic dimension. Because Chinese and (later) other Asian migrants were the first to experience these exclusive practices and policies in the Americas, the focus will be on this group in particular, keeping in mind that these dynamics affected other groups as well. Although this study will refer to examples from the Spanish empire, it will mainly focus on the era of exclusion that started approximately in the mid-nineteenth century and lasted until the mid-twentieth century, which was a period in which the discrimination of Chinese was especially extreme and extensive.

The hypothesis of this study is that the immigration of people who the elite (and other classes) consider to be ethnically, religiously and culturally inferior to the receiving societies was not only accepted, their voyage to the Americas was avidly promoted as long as the receiving society could control these immigrants and exploit their labor productivity. So it is believed that while the African slaves or Asian coolies (fooled by deceitful contracts) were taken in a forceful way, they were welcomed by the elites who benefited from their labor. This is due to the logic of exploitation and extractivism that required cheap, obedient labor to maximize profits, subjecting the workers to terrible living conditions.

However, if these individuals wanted to immigrate to the Americas on their own free will in search of a better life, they were often only permitted if they lived up to the expectations of the dominant groups in the receiving societies. If they were too economically successful in a certain sector or when they tried to occupy social spaces they weren't conceded, they frequently risked being discriminated, persecuted or even being killed. They were therefore no better off than those who had been able to free themselves from the yoke of slavery or (in the case of the contracted coolies) those who had been liberated by fulfilling their contract.[4] It is believed that upon immigrating on one's own free will, 'non-white' immigrants in the Americas were much more vulnerable to the risk of being discriminated and persecuted than 'white' immigrants. Therefore, it is believed that there is a correlation between mobility, liberty, and ethnicity. This correlation concerns both voluntary immigrants, and liberated slaves and coolies, at least during the period of exclusion. An analysis of the discrimination of Chinese in the Americas must therefore take into account the dynamics of the control over labor, mobility, and ethnicity that were at work against the background of racist and xenophobic attitudes. This will serve to better understand the cycles of discrimination that immigrants who are considered 'non-white' continue to suffer from today in the USA, Europe and other parts of the world.

If the first objective of this study is the description of the dynamics of the discrimination and exclusion of Chinese immigrants in the Americas, the second is to make visible the strategies that many of them were able to develop to cope with direct hatred and structural exclusion. Therefore, this study will not just describe cases of xenophobia and racism, it will try to emphasize the multiple ways to confront these phenomena, be it through resistance, organizations, or mutual aid networks.

The treatment of Chinese and other Asian immigrants in the Americas, which confronted them with multiple mechanisms of regulation, discrimination, and exclusion on the part of the authori-

---

4 This study will go into more detail on the discussion about a possible definition of 'voluntary' and 'forced', see especially chapter 3.3. It can already be said, however, that the degrees of freedom are an important marker not only to examine the transition from forced to paid labor, but also to examine the correlation between the control that the elite had over the work force and the regulation of immigration. It is in this sense that there also seems to be a correlation between the increase in voluntary labor in the Americas and the discrimination of free immigrants whose business success was feared by the labor movement.

ties and individuals working for the Spanish crown and the young Latin and North American republics seem to have a common thread through the centuries. On the one hand, this invites us to study upon which legal regulations the strategies and migratory practices depended. On the other hand, which forms of translocal and trans-regional action that these migrants developed that influenced the negotiation of practices of belonging and processes of nation state building need to be examined.

An interesting aspect is that certain patterns to justify discriminatory practices seem to have been repeated time and again. There are innumerable stereotypes, such as the economic competition of the Chinese, their supposed inability to adapt to the culture of European origin, and the adscription of degenerate racial features, a perverted character or claiming they carry contagious diseases. In contrast, Chinese immigrant communities frequently developed a high degree of resilience, adaptation to local conditions, understanding of the mechanisms of social, political, and economic organization, the organization of mutual aid associations, and of the will to socially and culturally adapt, which has led to the adoption of new religions, nationalities, and cultures. During the colonial era there were already examples of exclusion and adaptation, which will be dealt with in further detail in the following chapter.

2. The Period of the Manila Galleon: Chinese and Spaniards in the Philippines

With the beginning of the Iberian expansion there was continuity and transfer of the practices of the Reconquista, which ended in 1492 in the case of the Spanish crown with the defeat of Granada, to the Americas. In order to better understand the origins of the methods of control, violence, and exclusion that were to be used in the future colonies, it is worth briefly revisiting the transfer of concepts, which would now be considered racist, from the European Middle Ages to the period of exploration, conquest and the first European colonization in the Americas.

In medieval Spain, pre-existing concepts and methods of discrimination were reformulated in the concept of *'limpieza de sangre'*, or 'purity of blood.'[5] This concept was rooted in the accusation and persecution of Jews, which first came about at the pan-European level with the outbreak of the plague in the thirteenth and fourteenth centuries. After serving as the scapegoats, many Jews had to convert to Christianity. These converts, or new Christians, were suspected of still adhering to their Jewish faith, which is why they were referred to as 'crypto-Jews.' The old Christians used the concept of purity of blood to differentiate between them and the converts. According to Martínez, the concepts of race, casts and lineage that arose from this process were used during the Spanish Reconquista against converted Jews and Muslims and later transferred to the Americas, where they were adapted to the local conditions during the conquests and colonization (Martínez 2008, 28 and passim).[6]

With that, new visions of the 'other' (Todorov 2010) were created that were rooted in concepts of aversion toward the other during the Middle Ages, especially on the part of Christians in Europe

5 According to Bruns, the term 'race' was first used in Romance languages in the thirteenth century and became more frequently used starting in the sixteenth century (2013, 213).

6 See also Zúñiga (1999), and for a bibliography on the topic of 'converts' see Montes Romero-Camacho (2008).

and the Mediterranean against Muslims during the Crusades and the Reconquista. In the excellent introduction to her work about the expansion of the global space and the perception of the foreign from the Middle Ages to the Early Modern era, German medieval historian Kerstin Hitzbleck points out that while 'the foreign' in the sense of something yet unknown is "a neutral category of incomprehension" (2015, 6), this must be differentiated from 'the other'; the former implies a certain level of understanding, at least from the point of view of the perceiver. Even "the description as foreign is a part of the process of knowledge and appropriation that puts something that until now was unknown in relation with the familiar, making it describable and conceivable" (ibid., 5). Nevertheless, "what is described as foreign is included in the world view of the observer, but it avoids application [...]. With this respect, it is impossible for the observer to be aware of his own being. [...] The decisions to include and exclude are made by the observer" (ibid., 6).

Here there is a vision of the creation of the other on the part of the observing subject, but not on that of the observed. So it is a unidirectional perspective, not one of a process of transculturation and mutual learning that characterize any given cultural contact and exchange. It is not surprising, therefore, that these racist concepts were a part of the Spanish ideology at the time of the conquest of the Philippines in the sixteenth century.

The Philippines were conquered by the conquistadores led by Miguel López de Legazpi between 1565 and 1571 and they became part of the Viceroyalty of New Spain as the Captaincy General of the Philippines[7], which later included Guam, the Caroline Islands, Palau, and the Mariana Islands. A new dynamic began with the conquest and incorporation of the East and West Indies, and the Spanish Empire in the Americas. The expansion to Asia meant coming into contact with cultures and powers that could not be conquered, especially the great Empires of China and Japan. This made the Philippines in general and Manila in particular a frontier space for

7 According to Valladares, the Philippines acted "as a subcolony of New Spain" (2001, 36).

the Spanish Empire. Not only Spaniards and different Philippine ethnic groups interacted in this contact zone, but there were also Chinese who were usually involved in trading.

This was due to the establishment of a permanent marine route between Manila and Acapulco with the Manila Galleon and the establishment of extensive transpacific trade between the Viceroyalty of New Spain and the Empire of China. The silver from New Spain that the Spanish used to buy silk and valuable garments, porcelain, spices, and other objects from Chinese merchants (especially those from the Fujian province and Southeast China) was highly valued in all of Asia. According to Cano Borrego, the silver constituted "the foundation of trade with China, Japan, India and the larger islands of the Indonesian Archipelago. The Spanish piece of eight was accepted in practically every port of the Orient" (Cano Borrego 2016, 101). Manila soon turned into an important global market, the Spanish, Chinese, and Filipinos being the traders.[8]

While Spanish traders secured transpacific trading,[9] Chinese merchants (mainly Hokkien communities of Fujian) used pre-established maritime trading routes in the Nanyang or the South China Sea between Manila, China and Southeast Asia (T'ien 1989; Wang 1990; Lin 1990), especially starting in 1580: "When the Iberian crowns united in 1580, Manila was integrated in a trading network

8 Here, 'Filipino' refers to the great majority of the inhabitants of the Philippines, the indigenous of that time who the Spanish referred to as '*indios*'. At the end of the eighteenth century, '*filipino*' meant a Creole born in the Archipelago to Spanish parents (García de los Arcos 1999, 57).

9 This was connected with inter-American networks that connected Acapulco with Mexico City, Puebla, and Veracruz (and from there with the Caribbean and Spain, and with the port of Lima, Callao, from where goods and people were transported to the most distant parts of the Viceroyalty of Peru (Bonialian 2012). There was even a brief period at the end of the sixteenth century during which there was a direct route between Manila and Callao (Ruiz-Stovel 2009, 54), and also at the start of the seventeenth century (Vega Loyola 2017). For more on the history of the Manila Galleon see, for example, Yuste López (2007), Valdés Lakowsky (1987), Bonialian (2014), Bjork (1998), Flynn, Giráldez, and Sobredo (2001), Schurtz (1992).

that connected the Hindu ports of Goa and Diu with those of Malacca, Formosa and the trading post Macao" (Cano Borrego 2016, 101). Valladares adds: "Thanks to [Portuguese colonies in Africa, the Persian Golf, India, and China] [...] the Catholic Monarchy was able to spread its feared wings of universality and make it clear, in the words of Lope de Vega, 'you can walk all over the world through the lands of Philipp' [II]. [...] Asia was the Crown's most exquisite possession" (2001, 2).[10] The connection between the Iberian and Asian commercial networks gained significance on a global scale, interweaving Europe with Asia and the Americas, and the Manila Galleon went on to continue facilitating the flow of people, goods, and ideas for a quarter of a millennium.[11]

An image that represented the Spanish Empire as the leader and queen of Europe with its possessions in the Americas and Asia was produced in the eighteenth century in the masterpiece *Aspecto Simbólico del Mundo Hispánico* (1761) by the Filipino engraver Laureano Atlas.[12] It alludes to the popular representations of *Europa Regina* during the period of expansion of the Spanish Empire under Habsburg control, which can be seen in the engravings of various cartographic artists published in the sixteenth century (Bruns 2017; Schmale 2004). In each representation, the head of the queen with her crown represents Spain and Portugal. However, while the sixteenth-century works personifying Europe depict her body facing

---

10 Lope de Vega (1618. "La octava maravilla," 155. In Lope de Vega, *Décima parte de las comedias de Lope de Vega*. Barcelona: no ed.), quoted in Valladares.

11 For the history of the Philippines as a Spanish colony see, for example, Elizalde, Fradera, and Alonso (2001).

12 This was to illustrate the work *Theses de Mathematicas, de Cosmographia e Hidrographia* by Vicente de Memije. The complete title of the illustration is *Aspecto simbólico del mundo hispánico puntualmente arreglado al geográfico que a su glorioso católico rey D. Carlos Tercero el Magnánimo dedica y consagra don Vicente de Memije con IX theses y XC proposiciones que acerca de él defiende* (García Encina 2016, 222). See ibid., Morales Martínez (2016), and Díaz-Trechuelo (1962, 297-298) for an analysis of the work.

the east, Laureano Atlas' work is oriented toward the west, pointing to the Spanish overseas possessions, showing the empire as reaching from Europe to the other side of the world. Both personify Eurocentric imperial ambitions, but each with a different orientation, but the Filipino version, which was made to impress Bourbon King Charles III of Spain, was of global importance.

Laureano Atlas, *Aspecto Simbólico del Mundo Hispánico*, Manila 1761. Public domain. CC BY 4.0[13]

13 From *Theses Matemáticas de Cosmographia, Geographia y Hydrographía* by Vicente de Memije. https://upload.wikimedia.org/wikipedia/

2.1. The Philippines as an Axis of Global Trade and Space of Conflict, Sixteenth and Seventeenth Centuries

As mentioned above, the Philippines became a frontier space for the Spanish Empire,[14] and at the same time a space of transcultural contact and exchange, which would soon result in friction between the Spanish and other groups of interest, particularly the Chinese.[15] The visions of the 'other' with which the Spanish perceived Asian peoples had been conditioned through the habits and experiences of exclusion of Jews and Muslims, which had been acquired during the Reconquista in Europe, and of the indigenous in the conquest of American territories. According to Tremml-Werner, "such perceptions were encouraged through intentional othering of religious opponents and uneasiness about obvious cultural, political, and moral differences" (2015, 83). These images of "the other" facilitated and accompanied the execution of "several political agendas" (ibid.), which served the most important goal, being the imperial and ideological expansion (propagating the Christian faith). While the ideology in the Roman and Chinese empires were based on the concept of the superiority of their civilization, in the Spanish case a "strong notion of Christian superiority and Eurocentric self-aggrandisement" (ibid.) motivated their expansionist impetus and formed their relationships with 'the other.'

Chu states that the patterns of discrimination, persecution, and exclusion of Jews and Muslims in Europe went on to shape Spanish

---

commons/4/47/Laureano_atlas-aspecto_simbolico_del_mundo_hispanico.png. See also: Morales Martínez 2016, 686.

14 Tamar Herzog (2015) conceived imperial frontier spaces as a result of processes of territorial and social negotiations, Rahn Phillips (2007) analyzed the Spanish Empire according to the aspect of the maritime connections between the sixteenth and eighteenth centuries, and Matsuda (2012) conceptualized the Pacific as a transcultural and decentralized space. For a closer look at the concept of space of the Pacific Rim, see Dirlik (1998), for the concept of transculturation, see Pratt (2008).

15 For more on the concept of contact zones see Windus and Crailsheim (2013).

attitudes and practices toward the Chinese (Chu 2010, 55, note 5). It must be added that these attitudes were also directed toward the Moro, an important group of people in the southern islands of the Philippines who were Muslims mainly living in Mindanao and Jolo (Phelan 2011). During the same period, the Portuguese considered them to be a part of the "so-called 'infected races': Jews, Moros and Blacks" (Valladares 2001, 15). The Spanish crown organized expeditions to "*punish, repress, restrain, persecute [and] contain* [sic]" those who qualified as pirates that assaulted them on the sea and on land nearly everywhere in the Philippines (Mallari 1989, 412).[16] The trade between China and Manila started in 1567, just as the Spanish were conquering the Philippines. The Empire of China had previously maintained a strict policy of prohibiting access to the ocean in order to counteract contraband and piracy, the so-called policy of "*Haijing*, literally 'sea ban'" (Ollé 2013, 314). In fact, this corresponded with the policies of migration control that were prevalent in Europe at the time:

> In the Early Modern era, under prevailing conditions of demographic scarcity, for the European mercantilist and bellicist state acquisition and retention of human capital for economic production and war was a basic source of power; from this perspective, the most important form of control pertained to outward movement. Accordingly, unauthorized emigration was tantamount to treason and punishable by death or enslavement. (Zolberg 1999, 82)

For the Spaniards Manila was not only the door to China and Japan, it was the "entrepôt" (Cheong 1971) par excellence of this meeting and interlacement. This example highlights the reaches, limits, and contradictions of the Spanish crown's efforts to regulate and exclude Chinese immigrants, who the Spaniards referred to as *Sangleyes*. At the time this term likely originated from the Chinese expression *shanglai* 商来, which meant 'those who came to trade,' from *sengli* 生理, which meant 'trade' in the Fujian dialect, or from *changlai*

---

16 To get a captivating and detailed idea of this disputed space see Warren (2007).

常来, 'those who come frequently' (Ollé 2013, 316, note 9; Ollé 2013a, 156-157, note 2). As various studies have shown, the cooperation on the part of these traders was key in the success of transpacific trade, for the Spanish were unable to gain direct access to Chinese domestic trade and products (Ollé 2013a; Albiez, Kauppert, and Müller 2007). In contrast to the Portuguese, not only did the Spanish have no control over the seas between the Philippines and China, they were also unable to permanently establish themselves as the Chinese traders did.[17]

Businessmen from the Fujian province were in control of trade between Manila and Fujian, and the lucrative trade with the Spanish contributed to massive immigration of Fujianese to Manila. Before the arrival of the Spanish in the 1560s there was only a small community of a few hundred Chinese in Manila. However, those few, who were of the *hokkien* ethnicity, were prosperous (De Sousa Pinto 2013, 61). Within ten years of the establishment of the Manila Galleon, 5,000 Chinese had established themselves in Manila and it is estimated that by the beginning of the seventeenth century, this number had risen sixfold to around 30,000 Chinese (Ollé 2013, 315-316) and more than 3,000 Japanese (Cano Borrego 2016, 214). According to Ch'en (1968), at the time there were thirty Chinese men and women to each Spaniard.[18] Many of those who settled in the Philippines at the time were artisans and retailers who quickly monopolized these services. The majority of them were temporary, male residents who planned on returning to their families in China after having achieved the socio-economic advance they aimed for. However, this community was not characterized by "the social stability [...] often found among family-based settlers [...]" (Wickberg 1997, 155).

17 See Ollé 2002. Portugal achieved this with respect to Macao. For more on their presence in Asia see Ptak (1987) and De Sousa Pinto (2013). Russell-Wood (1992) wrote about the history of the Portuguese expansion from a global perspective. For a general overview of Chinese encounter with 'the West' see Mungello (2009).

18 For microhistoric approximations see Chia (2006) and Amyot (1973). For an analysis of local structures in Southeast China see Ownby (1993).

A Sangley couple in Manila around 1590. Public domain.[19]

As a method of controlling the Sangleyes from Manila, the then governor or the Philippines Gonzalo Ronquillo de Peñalosa established the first Chinatown of the Americas in 1580 (Carrillo 2017, 52). It was outside the Spanish colony (Intramuros), whose Fort Santiago pointed its canons toward this Chinese ghetto and market (Alejandrino 2003, 6). Decades later, in 1641, governor Sebastián

19 "Sangley in Boxer Codex." https://upload.wikimedia.org/wikipedia/commons/3/34/Sangley_in_Boxer_Codex.jpg. The original image can be found in the manuscript at Indiana University, also in a digitized version: *Sino-Spanish codex (Boxer codex)*, ca. 1590, fol. 204. Boxer mss. II. Indiana University, Bloomington, Indiana.

Hurtado de Corcuera explained this as a form of control against rebellions: "It was necessary to fence them in their Parian so that in case of any movement, from the turrets of the wall they could be secured and not leave to join the workers of the fields and other haciendas" (Gil 2011, 143, note 135). When it was first built it was called an *alcaicería*, but the Tagalog verb *parian* was soon adopted and its use extended through the Americas as a word describing a market where Asian products were traded (Sales-Colín Kortajarena 2016, 97). Carrillo points to the diversity of occupations among the Chinese inhabitants:

> The inhabitants are merchants, artisans, doctors, gardeners, silversmiths, embroiderers, fishers, bakers, bricklayers, builders, and people of many other occupations that quickly dominated the Manilan economy and the exchange with Fujian, to the point where they became key figures that supported the Spanish presence in the Philippine archipelago. (2017, 52)

The relationships between and within the diverse groups that lived in the Philippines were frequently characterized by conflict. As Kueh (2014) was able to show, close collaboration between the Spanish and Chinese was absolutely necessary for the economic success of the Spanish colonial project. The negotiation process between these groups often failed, however, which can partly be attributed to the fact that the colonial project in the Philippines did not proceed under the same conditions as in the Americas. According to Ollé, the relationships between the Spanish and Chinese resulted in "an ambivalent process, commercially very intense but greatly socially and institutionally unstable, where the mercantile logic conflicted with the Spanish missionary and imperial logic [...]" (2007, 28). Wickberg thinks that this tension between the necessity of coexistence and fear of revolts produced "a compromise in Spanish policy between economic interest and political security" (2001, 8). Furthermore, during the first thirty years of colonial domination, the Spanish in the Philippines had to be aware of "the real weakness of the position of the Spanish colony in the Philippines in the Asian context" (Ollé 2007, 27), especially with respect to the threat of Japanese, Dutch, and British invasion as well as Chinese pirates. According to Folch, regarding the last two, the Spanish "had no idea of the amount of piracy in the waters of Southern China" (2007, 268) which was much more common than in the Caribbean. Therefore, when the Chinese pirate Limahon (or Lim Ah Hong, in Mandarin Lin Feng) attacked Manila in 1574 with a fleet of 62 ships, the Spanish were very surprised (ibid., 270).[20]

Tensions soon increased. In 1593, 250 Chinese from Quanzhou, who had been forcibly recruited by the then Philippine governor Gómez Pérez Dasmariñas to serve as oarsmen in the conquest of the Maluka Islands, did not want to accept their destiny: Preferring death over the unfamiliar, cruel treatment by the foremen, they started a mutiny on the night of October 25th, taking over the flagship and killing the governor and the majority of the Spanish crew. The governor's son, Luis Pérez Dasmariñas, took revenge with the help of the Fujian authorities. A few months later, a Chinese imperial delegation arrived in Manila, supposedly in search of Chinese who had immigrated without permission. The Spanish interpreted this visit as a possible attempt to invade or gather reconnaissance (Borao 1998, 24-25), which was a sort of prelude to what was to occur ten years later.

The uncertainty and mistrust of the few Spanish who governed the colony resulted in a much more extreme reaction. It is estimated that at the time there were around 30,000 Chinese and only about 300 Spanish living in Manila; this number would never exceed 2,000 throughout the seventeenth century (Carrillo 2017, 53). In

20 In fact, the majority of Chinese pirates had previously been traders before starting their illegal business. It can also be said that they were illegalized because the repressive method against smugglers, such as the execution of people who took up coastal trade with foreigners, significantly contributed to people's choice to operate illegally (Kung and Ma 2014, 510-511). Informal trading networks existed alongside formal ones, regardless of, or perhaps as a result of the strict limitations of the Empire of China's foreign policy (Ollé 2013, 315).

1603, a Chinese imperial delegation arrived in Manila from Fujian for an interview with the governor. The intention of the delegation was to verify rumors about a legendary mountain of gold that supposedly existed opposite the bay of Manila. According to Antonio de Morga, given the more than 100 men and the strange questions they asked, the Spanish began to suspect other intentions. As they were already aware of the threat of Japanese invasion, they began fortifying the city and mobilizing troops and war vessels. Especially the clergy suspected that, in the case of a Chinese invasion, the Sangley population would likely ally with the invaders (Ruiz-Stovel 2009, 48). As Kueh has analyzed, this was due to the failure of the intermediaries among the Sangley upper and middle classes:

> When the abuses of Spanish authorities became unbearable and threatening to the lives of those they governed, Chinese intermediaries could not maintain their legitimizing claims of mitigating the demands of the regime on behalf of Chinese workers and lost control of those under their supervision. (2014, 19)

This resulted in a massacre reaching dimensions of genocide that the Spanish, with the help of auxiliary Filipino and Japanese troops, committed against the Chinese inhabitants of Manila. With an estimated 23,000 Chinese deaths (Ruiz-Stovel 2009, 48), it was the biggest massacre of Chinese immigrants in all of Southeast Asia during the entire colonial period, even when taking into account the sadly infamous massacre committed by the Dutch in Batavia.[21]

Nevertheless, thousands of Fujianese were soon establishing themselves in Manila. According to Ollé, they were "prepared to risk starring in the next massacre" (2007, 46), and deduces that the factors of push and pull that motivated their decision, specifically "the migratory pressure in Fujian and the attractive trade in Manila"

21 In the massacre of Chinese committed by the Dutch in 1740 in their colony of Batavia, it is estimated that they killed around 10,000 people (Dharmowijono 2009, 62, 289-325). Also see Somers Heidhues (2009); Kemasang (1982). For more on the context of the previous decades see Blussé (1981; 1986, 73-96).

(ibid.) were tremendous. Some of the survivors maintained their economic aspirations, even if through informal economic networks, "which are always considered to be 'pirate' by their rivals" (Ollé 2009, 91). In 1639, the Chinese community had again grown to around 30,000 or 33,000 (Ruiz-Stovel 2009, 59; Chang-Rodríguez 2015, 84). That year, Chinese agricultural workers who had been forced to work under very severe conditions marched to Manila to protest. In the city, the local Chinese joined to protest the high tax rate. Given the revolt, the Spanish once again murdered thousands of Chinese, with estimates ranging between 20,000 and 24,000 deaths (Chu 2010, 55-56; Sugaya 2007, 51). Only ten years later, the Chinese community in Manila had again reached 15,000 inhabitants (ibid., 56). There were other massacres in 1662 and 1686, although not of the same magnitude (Alejandrino 2003, 5).

Chu notes that these forms of persecution and exclusion were not only the extreme expression of mechanisms of control and exclusion that accompanied Spanish colonial policies regarding the Sangleyes from the beginning: "If expulsion and strict regulation of their economic activity did not reduce or inhibit the numbers of Chinese, then more violent means were used" (Chu 2010, 55). Massacres were not the norm, but rather multiple measures to regulate the mobility of the Chinese and their labor:

> Due to their fear and distrust of the Chinese as a result of their historical experiences with non-Spanish and non-Christian peoples in the Iberian Peninsula, they issued several decrees calling for mass deportation of the Chinese. Such decrees were issued in 1686, 1744, and 1747. Restrictions on immigration and regulation of Chinese commercial and industrial activities also sought to control the number of Chinese immigrants. In 1605, for example, the number of Chinese allowed to enter the Philippines was limited to 6,000. Heavy customs duties amounting to three percent of the value of every shipment were also levied on the Chinese trader. Moreover, the Chinese residing in the Philippines were required to pay a per capita tribute of 86 reales or 8 pesos a year. Non-Christians were either deported or restricted in their movements and interaction with the locals. (Ibid.)

It was clear that the regulation of the Chinese population in the Philippines was a central issue of the colonial politics, as shown by the example of the "discourse and opinion that they did not care for the fact that the Chinese, who they called Sangleyes, inhabited or lived off the *asiento* in the Philippines".[22] Focusing on the otherness of the Chinese seems to have been the norm, as the following words by Brother Plácido de Angulo in the seventeenth century show, finding it scandalous that the Chinese so naturally acted as if they were the Spaniards' equals: "[...] being foreigners, the Sangleyes behave as if they were natives and could do anything; the Spaniards themselves, natives, do not know nor are they allowed to do anything, as if they were foreigners" (Gil 2011, 447). However, the ambivalence of the regulation while still needing the Chinese as a motor for the colonial economy complicated the coexistence and codependency of the Spanish and Chinese. Because the Spanish did not employ them in their businesses, nor as agricultural workers or in the mines, the deportation of the Chinese affected the development of the colony very negatively and caused an economic crisis (Chu 2010, 56).

With regards to coexistence, García-Abásolo points out that "[...] focusing too much attention on the uprisings of the Sangleyes and the reaction of the Spanish may give the impression of a different reality: the reality that looks at the efforts of both groups to understand each other, consciously accepting that a separated life is not viable" (2011, 242). Nevertheless, it seems that this idea tends to blur the differences that existed between the attitudes the Spanish had toward the indigenous Filipinos and the Sangleyes respectively. While they saw the Filipinos as subjects they could control and integrate through Christianization, their attitude toward the Sangley merchants was different: they constructed a suspicious 'other' or

22 *Juicio del papel escrito en Manila, en veinte y cinco de marzo de mil seiscientos y setenta y siete, sobre que no se permitan de asiento los sangleyes en las Islas Filipinas*, fols. 332-358, Archivo de la Provincia del Santísimo Rosario, series B, section Sangleyes, Documentos sueltos 1594-1730, in chronological order, doc. 30. Archive of the University of Santo Tomás, Manila.

'foreign' that wanted to maintain their own identity, not completely assimilating (regardless of Christianization), and that representing a socio-economic competition that could threaten the control over the colony. It was in this way that the treatment of the Sangleyes was similar to that of the Jews and Muslims in Spain after having converted to Catholicism, their loyalty to which was questioned (Wickberg 1997, 155).

2.2. Transpacific Asian Migration to Continental New Spain

The situation in mainland New Spain was quite different. Therefore, the majority of the Asian migration across the Pacific to the Americas was of forced character, as Seijas (2014) shows for the years 1580 to 1700.[23] Although Slack still goes by estimates between 40,000 to 100,000 Asians that could have arrived in Acapulco from Manila between 1565 and 1815 (2010, 8), more recent studies suggest a much smaller number. For the period between 1565 and 1700, Oropeza Keresey calculates that the number of Asians was 7,200 of which 5,000 were settled in New Spain (2007, 188). For the same period, Seijas gives a conservative estimate of at least 8,100 Asians that were transported as slaves (2014, 84).

The number was therefore much lower than that of the forced migration of the enslaved Africans: Seijas and Sierra Silva cite (from Palmer)[24] a minimum of around 10,000 enslaved Africans that were taken to New Spain between 1521 and 1639. Even after the end of the Portuguese settlement in 1640, which marked the beginning of the return of the mass slave-owning mode of production to the Greater Caribbean (Zeuske 2013, 217), around 4,500 of them arrived by the end of the seventeenth century (Seijas and Sierra Sil-

23 According to the table "Figure 2.2 Total Registrations of Asians in Mexico, 1591-1705" (Seijas 2008, 75), about two-thirds of all Asians who arrived in New Spain were slaves.

24 Palmer, Colin. 1976. *Slaves of the White God: Blacks in Mexico, 1570–1650*. Cambridge: Harvard University Press, no page no.

va 2016, 310, 312). Provided the reality of smuggling and due to the lack of more sources mentioned by Seijas, Carrillo concludes that a total of between 10,000 and 20,000 Asians (both free and enslaved) may have crossed the Pacific to continental New Spain between 1565 and 1815 (2015, 7). Of these '*chinos*' (which was a generalization for all Asians in continental New Spain), Chong estimates that no more than 1,000 were free Chinese (Sangleyes from the Philippines) (2013, 230-231). The rest came from the Philippines and all areas of the Portuguese Estado da Índia, and to a lesser extent from Japan, Java, China, Papua and Brunei (Oropeza Keresey 2011, 27).

A large part of the free Asian immigrants were members of the Manila Galleon crews. Oropeza Keresey estimates that between 1565 and 1700 there was a minimum of 3,360, most of them cabin boys and carpenters (2007, 60-61). These Asians who arrived as free persons, together with those who had been emancipated from the yolk of enslavement, formed a diverse and fascinating group of people in New Spain (Seijas 2014, 143-174). Some were able to reach important social and economic positions in the colony, such as mayor of the *chinos* or barber (Machuca Chávez 2009; Slack 2010). However, regardless of their wish to adapt, "they were never totally accepted by the Spanish society [...]. Furthermore, the Spanish continued discriminating against them despite acculturation. In the end, a great imbalance of power remained" (Seijas 2008, 208). This imbalance did not exist within the casts, with which these Asians formed multiethnic communities (Chang J. 2016, 36). For their part, nearly all upper-class Sangleyes only went to Acapulco to do business and did not settle in mainland New Spain.[25]

However, voluntary migration on the part of Asians between the Asian and American parts of the Spanish colonial empire during the Early Modern era was not very relevant in quantitative terms, although it seems to have picked up after the abolition of the en-

25 See the case of the Fujianese Eng Kang of Manila, later known as Juan Bautista de Vera after being baptized, who accumulated a fortune and traveled to Acapulco a number of times (Kueh 2014, 63). For a general idea of the Sangleyes' impact on New Spanish trade, see Chong (2013).

slavement of '*indios chinos*' in New Spain starting in the 1670s. (Seijas 2008, 73; Seijas 2014, 227-241).[26] Considering that "the majority of the Chinese in the Philippines were free" (Oropeza Keresey 2007, 40) and that (as seen above) their numbers repeatedly grew to more than 20,000, even reaching 30,000, it can be concluded that the Spanish were quite successful in hindering free Chineses' access to the continental part of the Americas.

2.3. The Philippines of the Eighteenth Century: Consolidation, Miscegenation and the Regulation of Migration

During the eighteenth century the colony gradually consolidated through its modes of economic, social and ideological regulation of the Chinese, especially through taxation, mobility regimes, Christianization and miscegenation between Chinese and Filipinas, which facilitated their settlement and cultural assimilation (Wickberg 2001, 9). Christianization played a key role in converting the ethnic group of 'disloyal' Sangleyes, who were considered to be the 'others' in colonial society (for both the Spanish and the indigenous Filipinos), into "Spanish subjects" (Sugaya 2007, 53). This included the twofold process of the Christianization of 'disloyal' Chinese and the expulsion of those who opposed the conversion. Although they accepted the Catholic faith, they were still accused of being opportunists who neither practiced nor internalized the Catholic faith (Escoto 1999, 52). Escoto compares them to the Muslims in Spain that had converted to Catholicism after the Spanish Reconquest, the so-called Moriscos:

> The Chinese could be compared best to the Moriscos. [...] Like the Chinese, they were considered indispensable to the Spanish economy, but remained an unassimilable minority and posed a major

26 The abolition was not due to humanist ideals, but rather to the pressure the enslavers from the Atlantic were putting on the Spanish monarchy to end the competition in the Pacific (Chang J. 2016, 36).

> problem to the Spanish crown. They were overtaxed, discriminated against, suppressed after various rebellions and became Christians to avoid expulsion. They were also rounded up herded aboard waiting vessels to transport them to Africa. Their mass expulsion began in 1609 and was completed in 1614. Of the 300,000 Moriscos, only about 10,000 managed to remain. (Escoto 1999, 51)

There had been intentions to expulse the Chinese from Manila since 1594, but when a royal order came to expulse the Chinese from the Philippines that year, the governor Dasmariñas understood that they "needed to retain, at least, a small number of Chinese for its economic services" (Wickberg 2001, 10). In order to obey the order, they evacuated the Parian in Manila and expulsed a large number of residents, but they also relocated "a group of prominent Chinese merchants and artisans" (ibid.) to Binondo, a neighborhood that had been recently established just for this purpose on the opposite shore of the Pasig River. Coupled with the assignment of a Dominican parish, the neighborhood became "a kind of acculturation laboratory" (ibid.) of Christianized Chinese. It can be observed that the Spanish crown went from one extreme to the other: tolerating massive immigration that stimulated economic development in the colony and an extreme reaction based on a perceived loss of control, which repeatedly ended in ethnic cleansing.

Detail from the *Carta hydrographica y chorographica de las Yslas Filipinas* by Pedro Murillo Velarde, engraved by Nicolás De La Cruz Bagay (1734). Courtesy of the Library of Congress, Geography and Map Division.[27]

For the next 150 years the royal decrees to deport Chinese back to China were rarely carried out (Escoto 1999, 52), just like the decrees to limit the number of Chinese residents in the Philippines (Wickberg 2001, 8). This changed during the second half of the eighteenth century when a new recentralization policy started that meant tightening "the most intense and direct ties between the [Iberian] peninsula and the [Philippine] archipelago" (García Gimeno 2017, 175), which was accompanied by an "intense rearmament of colonial power in the Philippines" (ibid.). This control was to ex-

27 Murillo Velarde, Pedro, and Nicolás de La Cruz Bagay. 1734. *Carta hydrographica y chorographica de las Yslas Filipinas: dedicada al Rey Nuestro Señor por el Mariscal d. Campo D. Fernando Valdes Tamon Cavallo del Orden de Santiago de Govor. Y Capn.* [Manila, no ed.] [Map] Library of Congress. https://www.loc.gov/item/2013585226/.

tend to increased population and migration regulation. In 1755, the governor Pedro Manuel de Arandía Santisteban tried to expulse all of the non-Christian Chinese from the Philippines because he was worried about their increasing control of the local economy (Sugaya 1994). Furthermore, the governor ordered for Parian to be burnt down, which was possibly the reason why Christian Sangleyes cooperated with the British when they proceeded to invade and occupy Manila between 1762 and 1764 (García de los Arcos 1999, 68). After the city recovered, the colonial authorities expulsed the Chinese who had cooperated with the British forces (Escoto 1999). According to the royal charter issued by Charles III on April 17, 1766, the Christian Sangleyes not only cooperated with the enemy and betrayed the Spanish crown, they were guilty of being disloyal to their religion (ibid., 53). This happened just before the 1767 expulsion of the Jesuits that took effect in the Philippines in 1768 (Descalzo Yuste 2015, 250).

With that there were almost no more Chinese living in Manila,[28] until the governor José Basco y Vargas ordered their readmission in 1778 in order to revive the economy within the framework of the Bourbon Reforms and New Spain's inclusion in the free market, which was enacted by King Charles III in 1778 (Sugaya 2007, 54). While contributing to economic development, the Spanish authorities were careful to maintain the "Catholic Filipinos" (ibid., 55). Starting in 1783, the Chinese were all legally obliged to have their license of residence (*radicación*) that proved their residential and fiscal registration. This doubled as a migration and economic control, which was accompanied by an intensification of ideological and social control measures through a decree that prohibited the practice of 'idolatry' among the Chinese, who at the time were almost all Christians (ibid., 55-56).

The population of Chinese-Filipino mestizos had considerably grown in number up to that point. From 1741 on, they represented a

28 However, Chu calculates that between 1750 and 1850 the number of Chinese in the Philippines was between 10,000 and 20,000 because they "found other ways to enter the Philippines" (2010, 57).

group that was big enough to be identified as an element that was distinct from Spaniards, Filipinos, and Chinese, and they formed their own separate fiscal group (Wickberg 2001, 12). According to the Jesuit Father Murrillo Velarde y Bravo, this group was irritable and "could cause discord in society" (ibid., 13). There is an image here taken from the famous 1734 map of the Philippine Islands for which Philip II designated Murillo Velarde himself to manage. There are four types of Sangleyes pictured here, they are in complete harmony, which could be interpreted as a reflection of the process of the advanced acculturation as perceived by the Spanish authorities. In 1734, the bloody confrontations of the previous centuries lay nearly two generations back, and yet the clashes between the Spanish and Sangleyes that marked the second half of the eighteenth century were yet to come.

Detail from the *Carta hydrographica y chorographica de las Yslas Filipinas* by Pedro Murillo Velarde, engraved by Nicolás De La Cruz Bagay (1734). Courtesy of the Library of Congress, Geography and Map Division.[29]

29 Murillo Velarde, Pedro, and Nicolás de La Cruz Bagay. 1734. *Carta hydrographica y chorographica de las Yslas Filipinas: dedicada al Rey*

At the beginning of the nineteenth century, around 120,000 Chinese mestizos formed five percent of the Philippine population, there being only around 4,000 Spaniards and approximately 7,000 Chinese (Chu 2010, 66, table 2). In the central provinces of Luzon this group even represented fifteen percent of the population. Not only were they the biggest minority in the Philippines, they were also a significant number of them among landowners and wholesale merchants (Wickberg 2001, 13-16). This all points to a transculturation process that also included the Chinese who were not of mixed race. After the turbulence that caused the persecution and deportation of the Sangleyes in the 1760s until their readmission the following decade, the adscription for Sangleyes began to change. Instead of classifying them according to their religious affiliation, the Spanish authorities began classifying them according to their residency status, although conversion to the Catholic faith continued to be an important element of colonial control. For example, it was a requirement for acquiring citizenship and marrying Filipinas. Furthermore, as part of the strategy to attract a certain number of Chinese for economic reasons, starting in 1790 the Sangleyes' poll tax was lowered from 81 to 54 reales annually, although the group continued to be taxed much more than the rest of colonial society (Chu 2010, 69, 73).

As a consequence of the wars of independence in New Spain, in 1815 the Manila Galleon's route to Acapulco was suspended, which brought an end to the shared history with New Spain for the next two and a half centuries. The history of the Philippines as a part of the Spanish colonial empire continued until 1898 when the United States took it away from both Spain and the Filipino independence fighters.

Nuestro Señor por el Mariscal d. Campo D. Fernando Valdes Tamon Cavallo del Orden de Santiago de Govor. Y Capn. [Manila, no ed.] [Map] Library of Congress. https://www.loc.gov/item/2013585226/.

Chapter 2 Summary

This study has so far shown how the history of the links between Chinese and Spaniards in the Philippines developed based on two principle axes: that of the economic development of the colony and that of political, economic, social and ideological control that the Spanish colonizers established and sought to maintain at all costs over these territories that represented an extreme minority. Apart from the indigenous Philippine subjects, Chinese merchants, artisans, and laborers were indispensable in order to develop the colony. But at the same time, the proximity to the Empire of China and the threat of other powers, such as the Japanese and Dutch, point to the risk the Spanish took with this colony. However, during the first 100 years of colonial domination in the Philippines they favored or at least tolerated the massive Chinese immigration for economic reasons, but they were strictly vigilant about the colony's external and internal security, not hesitating to ensure it using extreme repression when they felt threatened.

In the seventeenth century there was a process of miscegenation (mainly between Chinese men and Filipinas) and partial acculturation or 'integration' of Christian Sangleyes into the colonial sociocultural system. There was a simultaneous, significant decrease of Chinese immigration as it was more conditioned to immigration and residency regulations, especially starting with the application of Bourbon ideas and, eventually, reforms in the Philippines at the end of the century. The attitudes of the Spanish toward the Chinese seem to have a less ideological character and more of that of enlightenment (within the limits of Christian ideology), which also had a significant effect on the everyday interactions between the Spanish, the creoles, Sangleyes and Chinese mestizos.

In the sixteenth and part of the seventeenth century, practices of exclusion were marked by attitudes that stemmed from racist and xenophobic imaginaries that had been developing since the Middle Ages and that were transmitted to the Americas and Asia with the European expansion. From the eighteenth to the mid-nineteenth century these attitudes went from socio-moral and ideological control to a conception of control based more on territory, understanding a notion of mobility linked less to ethnicity and more to socio-economic status.

Regarding the transpacific Asian migration to New Spain and from there to other parts of the Americas, the numbers were not significant during the Early Modern era and the majority of those who migrated had to do so as an enslaved person. The only exception were the Philippines, which because of its the proximity to the rest of Southeast Asia and its distance from continental New Spain held a special status in the Spanish colonial empire with its own characteristics of co-dependence between Spaniards, Chinese and Filipinos. The next section of this study will take a look at the similarities and differences between this period and what happened in many parts of the Americas in the nineteenth and twentieth centuries.

3. Forced Migration and Voluntary Migration in the Modern Age

Before discussing Chinese migration to the Americas, which started on a larger scale in the mid-nineteenth century, the following will briefly outline the context in which these new migratory dynamics took place.

3.1. From the Age of Revolution to the Great Migrations

At the end of the eighteenth century and beginning of the nineteenth century, various processes came together that shook the foundation of the colonial system as established by European powers in the Americas and impacted migration regimes. The French and Indian War and the subsequent fiscal, administrative and economic reforms (called Bourbon Reforms in the Spanish Empire), the assertion of English dominion over the Spanish, the revolution and independence in the United States, and the French Revolution all started a cycle of reforms and revolutions that ended four decades later with the wars of independence in most Iberian colonies.[30] As a result, the majority of colonial territories became independent of their respective mother countries. The intention of the Creole elites in this context was to establish republics (except in the Brazilian case), continue developing free trade, and at the same time maintain control over the ethnic and social hierarchies that had been established by the defeated colonial powers.

A secondary cycle of revolutions began with the successful slave revolt in Saint-Domingue and its resulting independence in

30 This Age of Revolution spread through Europe between 1789 and 1848, see Hobsbawm (1995); for more current discussions see Bell and Mintzker (2018). Kossok (1985) proposed a different periodization to analyze the cycle of revolutions in Spain which shows that these are revolutionary cycles that can overlap, but that they each have their own relevance according to the scale of the focus (global, hemispheric, or regional).

1804 as Haiti. The result of this revolution against the white elite was that it was used as a negative example by the Creole elite elsewhere to show how dangerous it could be to allow enslaved Africans to rise up and demand equality. The Creoles feared a 'second Haiti', especially in the Caribbean where slavery was still part of the extractive system, both in the remaining colonies (such as Cuba and Puerto Rico) and in the new republics.[31] If the bourgeois revolutions,[32] which could include the Latin American wars of independence,[33] were seen "as a symbol of anti-imperial revolution" (Stinchcombe 1994, 3), the revolution in Saint-Domingue was considered "*a symbol of slave revolt*" (ibid., italics in the original), or a "fatality" (Munford and Zeuske 1988, 29). After gaining independence, Haiti continued this legacy and was discredited as a breeding ground for revolutionaries (which for a time it certainly was, considering it was one of the most notable examples of the era of Bolívar in Haiti). Having been the first country in the Americas to permanently abolished slavery, it experienced what was possibly the longest period of diplomatic and economic isolation at the hands of the great Western powers in all of nineteenth-century history.[34] It was not until the American Civil War and the abolition of slavery in the states of the Union that the United States officially recognized Haiti, which was formerly looked down on as "a symbol of antislavery and black equality" (Stinchcombe 1994, 4).

---

31 See González-Ripoll (2004); Gómez (2006); Munro and Walcott-Hackshaw (2006). For these and other results of the Haitian Revolution and the Caribbean see articles published in Geggus (2001).

32 Of course one could include other types of revolutions of this period, see Stern (1987) for an excellent overview.

33 For a critical evaluation of the revolutionary character of the wars of independence see Chust (2015).

34 According to Stinchcombe, they formed a great "reactionary diplomatic alliance against a black revolutionary republic" (1994, 2), and it was not until the 1830s and 1860s that the European governments and the republican governments in the Americas established diplomatic relations with Haiti (ibid.).

It is still, however, a lesser-known historical event. If in 1995 Trouillot confirmed the persistent "general silencing of the Haitian Revolution by Western historiography" (1995, 27), it is not surprising that there is even less known about the progressive thoughts of a Haiti that fought for the application of human rights for all human beings. It is interesting that at the heyday of colonial and racist ideas (in Europe) progressive thinkers and historians in the so-called Global South raised their voices to refute these ideas. In 1885, the same year in which European powers divided the African continent between themselves, Haitian anthropologist and politician Joseph-Anténor Firmin defended ideas of universal equality in his *De L'Égalité des Races Humaines* stating:

> [...] one of the roots of the mistake that really insults the intelligence of philosophers and anthropologists and that maintains the hypothesis of racial inequality is the prevailing influence of domineering and usurping aspirations of European policy, the main source of these aspirations being the spirit of domination and the proud faith in the superiority of the Caucasian man (1998, 474).

Firmin wrote this in a climate of absolute adversity, directly referring to people like Gobineau who postulated a supposed 'white' supremacy. Five decades later, while Nazi Germany was preparing for European invasion and the Holocaust, Marxist historian Cyril Lionel Robert James from Trinidad and Tobago published his book *The Black Jacobins* in 1938 (James 1980). There he highlighted the ideals that Toussaint l'Ouverture tried to transfer from the French Revolution to that in Saint-Domingue, the future Haiti. However, only the 1962 edition received wide reception in the context of the civil rights movement in the United States (Trouillot 1995,104).

With that, this study aims to point out the contradictory dynamics of the liberation of slaves by virtue of their own effort ('from below') and through abolition (or decreed liberation 'from above') that were marked by the white elite's desire to control people of a different color, which in Haiti caused a certain unexpected overlap of interests of abolitionists and those in favor of slavery. The following will show how the paternalistic control of free men 'of color' on the part of the elite in the Americas continued to be a constant, and that it extended to migration control.

3.2. The Coolie Trade – an Intermediate Step toward Voluntary Labor?

Although England had been defeated in its thirteen North American colonies, it continued expanding its imperial power over the seas and extended its influential power in other parts of the world, especially in Asia (Tomich 2016a). Wills attributes this increase in power in Asia to England's imposition to the detriment of the French, with whom they were practically fighting a World War from 1770 to 1815 (2014, 202). Because England no longer maintained control over the greater part of the slave territories in the Americas, they began withdrawing from their role in the Middle Passage, which had brought them and other European powers so much wealth through the slave trade. As England increasingly spread ideas of the Enlightenment and abolition – first with regard to slave trade and later to slavery itself – they gained more and more supporters. Rediker, Pybus, and Christopher argued:

> Drawing upon and publicizing the gruesome social conditions and the fierce resistance by enslaved Africans aboard the slave ships, the abolitionists managed to focus attention on a reality far beyond the shores of most people's experience and to make real the horrors of the middle passage to a metropolitan reading public. (2007, 1)

They aptly point out that the Middle Passage can be "[…] utilized as a concept – the structuring link between expropriation in one geographic setting and exploitation in another" (ibid., 2). This will later aid in the better understanding of the implications of the concept of the 'Yellow Pacific' that would be characterized by the coolie trade.

Beginning in the late eighteenth century, with its expansion in Asia and naval superiority, England started to "[a]ssemble a Pacific that would link commodities like opium and tea in India and China with the trade of agricultural commodities in the Americas and thus it inaugurated new forces for migration and demands for labor [...]" (Chang J. 2016, 37). This was to reactivate, transform and profoundly diversify the transpacific relationship between Asia and the Americas. Already weakened by the free trade as decreed by Charles III in 1778, the link between Manila and Acapulco, which lasted a quarter of a millennium, was finally broken in 1815 due to the wars of independence and Spain's difficult financial situation after the occupation by Napoleon (Valdés Lakowsky 1983). The weakening of Spanish power was taken advantage of by the British and other actors interested in transpacific trade, among them the United States and Germany. Within these new dynamics, the lascars (Indian sailors) were the first Asian group to cross the Pacific as a crew in European vessels under the British flag and, according to Chang, "British officials gradually constructed a global bureaucratic system of recruiting, exporting, and regulating contracted Indian and Chinese workers, or coolies" (Chang J. 2016, 38).

Trade of the coolies, workers contracted primarily in India and China, was a multi-national business that, in the light of the impulses the industrial revolution was giving to global production, tried to meet the demand for cheap and regulated labor in the Americas, Southeast Asia, Oceania, Australia, and South Africa in the second half of the nineteenth century. In the case of the Chinese, coolie trade was also the result of the competition between European and other powers for the control of the access to labor that can be dominated by forced exploitation:

> [It] situates the Chinese coolie trade as a confluence and siting of global rivalries and alignments involving European nations, the United States, Africa, and China, and the control of slave and coolie labors, with a particular rivalry taking place between Britain and Spain in relation to Cuba and sugar. (Yun 2008, 13)

The British reached a privileged position in this rivalry through the first Opium Wars against China, gaining control over Hong Kong, which was occupied in 1841 and conceded by China to Great Britain in 1843 in the Treaty of Nanking (Sinn 2013, 12). With that they also gained access to free trade in the most important Chinese ports – Canton, Amoy, Foochow (now Guangzhou, Xiamen, and Fuzhou), Ningbo, and Shanghai. Situated along the Pearl River near Canton and Macao, Hong Kong was in a strategically ideal location for transoceanic trade. In 1890, the German encyclopedia *Meyers Konversations-Lexikon* assessed the rise of Hong Kong and the relative decline of Canton as of 1841 from a Eurocentric perspective:

> C.[anton] is the cradle of European trade in China because trade with the West was concentrated here before the great Opium Wars with the British (1841). Because they have now dispersed to a number of contract ports, C. has lost much of its earlier importance, which in large part is due to the prospering English free port of Hong Kong. C. is nevertheless the most important city in Southern China. (*Meyers Konversations-Lexikon* 1890, 9, 474)

The following image is the map of the area that accompanied the above description.

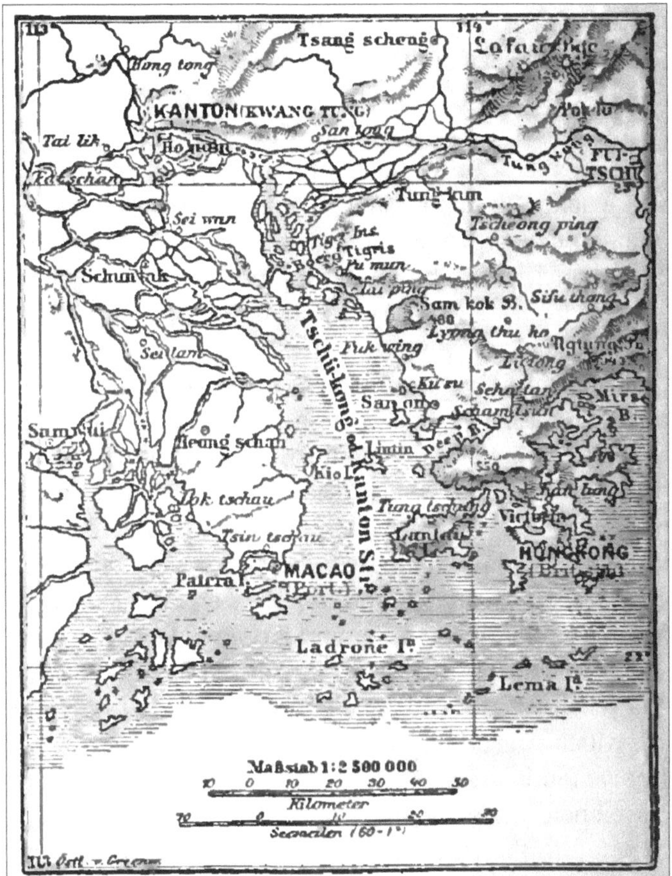

Situationskärtchen von Kanton, Makao, Hongkong.

Situationskärtchen von Kanton, Makao, Hongkong
(*Meyers Konversations-Lexikon* 1890, vol. 9, 474). Public Domain.

The result of the first Opium War was the opening of a new and powerful transoceanic transportation route, initially between China, the Indian Ocean, and the Atlantic, and soon expanding to the Pacific (Sinn 2013, 12). The Portuguese colony of Macao and British Hong Kong went on to competitively divide the lucrative trade of Cantonese, who embarked for the Americas in large numbers as coolies and voluntary migrants.

In the Americas, controllable labor was becoming scarce due to the abolition of slavery in the new Latin American republics, Haiti, and in the British Empire, and due to the increased demand for labor (in these republics as well as in those with continued slavery) that was caused by the development of industrial plantation economies, as well as guano extraction, and mining industries, among others. This capitalist development was accompanied by the expansion of new technologies that revolutionized infrastructure, such as the steam boat and railway, the construction of which demanded thousands and thousands of workers.

During the initial years of the *Trata Amarilla* (1847–1874),[35] approximately one and a half million people (almost entirely men) were recruited as coolies in the Southern Chinese province of Guangdong, often through trickery or by becoming indebted (Young 2014, 32; Hu-DeHart 2007, 167). After they were gathered in Macao (where they stayed in bunkhouses like slaves) and other ports like Amoy and were transported to the Americas on transoceanic voyages under inhumane conditions. The mortality rate was higher than during the slave trade: of the nearly one quarter of a million coolies that left China for the Americas (mostly to Cuba and Peru), 30,000 died on board, which was around 12% (Yun 2008, 7). The consequences were frequent mutinies, suicides, and other forms of resistance.

Approximately double the amount of coolies from India that were imported to the British, French, and Dutch colonies in South America and the Caribbean between 1838 and 1924 (Kumar Mishra 2009, 233) must also be added to this equation, however very carefully due to the large possible margins of error.[36] Here the time frame is believed to be different than in the case of the trade of Chinese coolies because the latter abruptly ended in 1874. This halt oc-

35 Yun states that the first experiments with coolie trade took place as early as the seventeenth century by the Dutch in their American colonies (2008, 5). The first delivery of coolies by the British was in 1806 to the British colony of Trinidad in the Caribbean (Chang-Rodríguez 2015, 87).

36 Regarding the issues the British authorities had when quantifying the Hindu immigrants in Ceylon see Look Lai (2009, 29-30).

curred when the Empire of China intervened after sending a commission to investigate the abuse of Chinese workers who had been contracted in Cuba by the Spanish crown. This dispute of the Qing government was eventually supported by nearly all of the great European powers (England, Russia, France, and Germany) and the United States (Ng 2014, 41).[37] From the beginning of the trade, there were multiple forms of resistance toward maltreatment during the voyage as well as on the job site, and they were similar to those used by African slaves, with the exception being that the number of suicides among the Chinese seems to have been higher than among enslaved Africans (Young 2014, 34-41).

In the case of the Chinese coolies, almost all of them were *punti* 'natives' (本地, *bendi* in Mandarin) and *hakka* 'visitors' (客家, *kejia*) from seven counties of the Guangdong (then Canton) province. Before embarking in the Chinese ports that were controlled by the Europeans, they signed an eight-year contract that was written in Chinese and Spanish. But the conditions of recruitment (often through deception), transport (under the same or worse conditions than the slave trade), and labor (almost always as cruel as that of the African slaves) made the lives of coolies more similar to slavery. However, even though there were numerous attempts on the part of the temporary owners to extend the contracts to make them unlimited, there were thousands of coolies that managed to survive the duration of their contract and went on to start a life in the receiving societies.

For many years, research on the trade of contracted Asian workers has argued that this phenomenon was mostly due to the abolition of slavery, an institution that it replaced.[38] But while this

---

37 The migration of Chinese coolies to other parts of the world also does not fit into the periodization of the *Trata Amarilla* to the Americas. Harris notes that between 1904 and 1910, the colony of Transvaal (South Africa) imported 63,695 Chinese to work in the gold mines, while in the colony Natal 152,184 Hindus were imported between 1860 and 1911 (2010, 147).

38 Meagher wrote of "[t]he phenomenon of indentured labor, which followed upon the abolition of slavery [...]" (2008, 21).

was certainly true in some cases,[39] it is known today that the abolition of slavery and coolie trade were two processes that overlapped and often complemented each other. In the United States, Cuba, and Brazil, slavery was even extended and persisted until 1863, 1886, and 1888 respectively.[40] This meant that – for lack of legal ways to import slaves – the smuggling of slaves across the Atlantic would grow exponentially as part of what Tomich (2016), Laviña and Zeuske (2014), and other scholars call the 'Second Slavery', which meant a "systemic redeployment and expansion of Atlantic slavery during the nineteenth century" (Tomich and Zeuske 2008, 91).[41] With reference to Luiz Felipe de Alencastro, Marques accurately notes that this forced transport from Africa of "individuals illegally enslaved in the Americas" could be considered "one of the greatest crimes of the nineteenth century" (2016, 173). This refers to a legal framework of the period because the slave trade continued for decades after it had been prohibited in the United States (1807), Cuba (1820), and Brazil (1850). Of the approximately twelve million slaves that were transported during the transatlantic slave trade in total, some two million slaves were transported to these regions during this Second Slavery (Zeuske 2013, 456-457).

Zeuske links the coolie trade with his concept of the "*Hidden Atlantic*" (ibid., 28)[42] and postulates that the discourse on the nineteenth century as a 'centennial of abolition' ignores the incredible dynamics of exploitation that governed not only the Atlantic, but

39 Like the Hindu coolies in the British Empire (Lal 1996, 168).

40 This could also be framed within a second cycle of revolutions and changes that profoundly affected the plantation system in the world of the Atlantic between the decades of 1860 and 1896 (Dal Lago 2009, 393).

41 Also see Tomich (2016) and Laviña and Zeuske (2014). This process can be described as follows: "The transformation of historical capitalism in the long nineteenth century was marked by the expansion of slavery not only in Brazil and Cuba, but also in the United States [...]" (Marques 2016, 173-174).

42 Italics in the original.

also the Indian and Pacific Oceans and that mobilized millions of people. However, whether or not the coolie trade had more of a forced character or the character of free migration is still an issue of debate. While Young summarizes the current status of this complex discussion (2014, 46-50), he doesn't delve into other interpretive frames. He basically goes along the same line as Rodríguez Pastor, who described the case of Peru by simply saying that the Chinese coolies arrived as "semi-slaves" (2005, 447). Yun critically discusses the concept of 'transition' from indentured work (slave labor) to free labor in various dimensions and warns that the application of this concept reduces the Asian workers to intermediate objects instead of subjects (2008, 1-5). Boatcă even goes as far as to say that we are "asking the wrong question" (2013, 287) if the discussion is limited to binary interpretations. Referencing Tomich, she maintains that this way of thinking hinders the discovery of "important historical connections between, and continuities among, labor regimes usually constructed as polar opposites" (ibid.).

We are conscious of these problems and understand that the trade of Asians was not a mere step in the supposedly progressive and teleological transformation of modes of exploitation from the control of production to 'free' and paid labor, parallel to the "liberation" of the individual from the yoke of feudalism and the emergence of the citizen who voluntarily participates in the development of nation states that resulted from the bourgeois revolutions. The coolie trade was rather a part of the changing extractivist system in the nineteenth century, in which the relevance of the distinction between 'free' and 'forced' workers became blurred as the need for an intersectional analysis of the structural continuity of exploitation and the asymmetries of social, ethnic, political, and gender power relations. Therefore, it is of special interest to study the events that transpired at the beginning of the era of voluntary and 'free' mass migration. In order to analyze free migration of Chinese to the Americas, it is necessary to briefly outline the problem of the meaning and implications of the disjunctive 'free' vs. 'forced' with reference to migration in order to gain more conceptual clarity.

3.3. What is Free Migration?

For the purpose of this study it is helpful to think of the implications that arise when analyzing the forced, voluntary or free characters of migration and their limits. Continuing with the intention of emphasizing the agency of migrants that make the decision to move to a distant land for a prolonged period of time, we prefer to use the term 'free migration.' This links up with the definitions of historians that work with migration and tend to define it according to two poles of free migration and its opposite: forced migration.[43] As stated above, this does entail problems, especially when migrants are reduced to mere objects because of their status as adscribed by others and their desires and decision-making space are disregarded.

In the case of the coolies, it has already been said that the issue is very complex, and at the start of the era of mass 'free' migration to the Americas beginning around 1830, it becomes even more complicated. Eltis refers to the "[…] intermediate status of indentured and contract migrants" (2004, 314) who obtained a free transoceanic passage in exchange for control over their labor for a period limited by the contract they signed. But their situation was ambivalent: "Because they entered into a contract more or less voluntarily, they were like free migrants, and because they could be bought and sold and did not have much control over this process, or the work they were required to perform during the indenture, they were like slaves" (ibid.). Eltis identifies a key element to approaching migrants as subjects and agents of their own destiny by establishing the category of forced migrants as those who did not want to be captured and forcibly relocated: "migrants [...] unwilling to relocate" (ibid.). The inverse conclusion is therefore that the primacy of the free will to migrate is a fundamental element of 'free migration'. The most recent edition of the *Glossary on Migration* by the United Nations' International Organization for Migration (IOM) has written the following under the rubric 'forced migration':

43 See Emmer (2004) and several articles in Eltis (2002), especially Look Lai (2002) and Eltis (2002a and 2002b).

> A migratory movement in which an element of coercion exists, including threats to life and livelihood, whether arising from natural or man-made causes (e.g. movements of refugees and internally displaced persons as well as people displaced by natural or environmental disasters, chemical or nuclear disasters, famine, or development projects). (*Glossary on Migration* 2011, 39)

The glossary does not, however, make any reference to the opposite, which is likely due to the problems that arise when looking for a definition of free movement. Even though it is now the 21st century, the IOM does not consider forced migrants to be unfree people.[44] But they gave a new meaning to coercion: it treats migrants like victims of events and adverse conditions that cause them to migrate. Consequently, international law specialist Achiume (2018) has introduced the term "involuntary migration" (2018, 335, note 2). This definition creates a category that does not only include refugees, but "the category extends to include coerced movement that is not legally protected by international law" (ibid.).

This adds a new dimension to the meaning of the paradigm of will that was mentioned above. The IOM has once again denied migrants the power to decide and act, and ascribed them the status of victims, which ultimately grants them the necessary legitimacy to migrate. That means they migrate against their own will, or their will is not determined by a personal or free decision, but by things they cannot control.[45] Achiume attempts to expand the reaches of protection for migrants and adds "extreme economic hardship" (ibid.) to the list of reasons that justify migration, although it is not protected by law. By proposing the recognition of economic rea-

44 Despite the continued forms of non-institutionalized slavery and human trafficking that still exist today; see Zeuske (2013, 1-3; 567-573).

45 We will not go into detail on the development of this concept, but just mention that its origins are in the emphasis put on the protection of refugees and displaced people as a consequence of the Second World War as expressed in the Geneva Convention on the state of refugees adopted in 1951 and extended to non-European countries in a 1967 protocol (Betts and Kainz 2017, 2).

sons, Achiume is trying to include economic refugees among legitimate migrant groups, for which her term "involuntary migration" (ibid., 335) serves as an instrument to create more protection for, and acceptance of, migrants. Both Achiume's and the IOM's definition leave a large margin of interpretation with respect to what is understood as an "element of coercion" (*Glossary on Migration* 2011, 39) as the driving force of migration, probably in order to be relevant for many different kinds of migration.

The problem with this approach in the context of this article's focus, again, is that it denies the migrants' agency and treats them like objects within a process or a context of coercion that forces them to migrate; it is only under these conditions that they can legitimately move, being required to present evidence of the necessity to migrate as accepted by the gatekeepers who regulate access within migratory regimes. In the present case, it is fitting to apply the notion of 'voluntary' to the 'free' Chinese immigrants. We think it serves to distance them from slaves who were transported against their will, as well as from coolies who were lured into slave-like working conditions through deception and false promises, although, unlike slavery, it was only for a foreseeable amount of time.

In emphasizing the ability to make decisions about one's destiny, migrants and their desires, wishes, and worries play a key role in the analysis of migration and its causes.[46] Theories of other phenomena are also applicable to the analysis of the decision-making space within which they make the decision to migrate, for example, the study of social movements. According to Kriesi, people decide to move according to the political opportunity structures that provide the framework for the movements (2004, 80). By drawing parallels with the migratory process, the concept of opportunity structures also influences the options that migrants take into account when immigrating, emigrating, or re-migrating.

---

46 See Hoerder (2002), especially subchapter 1.3 (Migrants as Actors and a Systems Approach).

Far from rejecting the usefulness of analytic parameters (such as that of the IOM) that help identify the level of pressure felt by migrants, this pressure can also be coupled with the notions of attraction, expectations, life strategies, and habits that communities and transnational networks of migrants have developed. On the one hand, the wide variety of theories on migration include many foci that are doing just that,[47] on the other hand, they also present a new situation of populist and xenophobic tendencies that affect the direction of studies on migration.[48]

In this sense, Glick Schiller and Salazar present contemporary currents in the study of mobility that postulate that one can study any type of mobility – be it forced or voluntary – using the same angle. They point out that some research questions the use of distinctions that typically made regarding the duration of mobility, meaning the differences between the mobility of people who migrate and settle for a prolonged period, and stays of medium or short durations (for study, work, tourism, etc.). However, they indicate that "the current global economic crisis seems to be accompanied by a normalization – once again – of national borders and ethnic boundaries [...]" (2013, 184). By "once again" the authors seem to be referring to the establishment of these boundaries in the nineteenth century and the rise of nationalism and nativistic, xenophobic, and racist attitudes, which is comparable to what is happening today: "Demagogues and national security experts now look askance at many of those who move, defining mobility as dangerous and threatening, while immobility is seen as normal and necessary for political and personal security" (ibid.). We agree with this observation, which also coincides with the necessity to broaden the view of dynamics of exclusion that develop with the foundation of

47 See articles in Amelina, Faist, and Nergiz (2016), especially Amelina and Faist (2016); Glick Schiller (2012). See also Bauböck and Faist (2010) and the approaches that are still relevant for the United States in Hirschman, Kasinitz, and DeWind (1999), particularly Portes.

48 See Zapata-Barrero (2018); DeWaard (2015); Achiume (2018 and 2014).

nation states in order to understand and contextualize the new and troubling reality at present.[49]

From a broader perspective on migratory processes at the global level, Lucassen, Lucassen, and Manning, in agreement with Eltis, maintain that in order to "overcome the unproductive free–unfree dichotomy" (2010, 10), it seems useful to be aware that "[...] most migration has both voluntary and coercive elements, which are difficult if not impossible to disentangle" (ibid.). However, the diversity of case studies on migration have shown that it is in fact valuable to try to identify and analyze the main factors of both migration and what guides and frames it and compare them with the consequences of the decisions that are made.[50]

3.4. Asian Immigration as a Part of the Free Migration to the Americas

Studies on global migrations today are in agreement with McKeown's proposal that between the 1840s and 1940s, migrations reached an especially high level: an estimated total of 149 to 161 million people migrated during this period, and of these, between 55 and 58 million arrived in the Americas coming from Europe (2004, 156). If the period of the Second Slavery is added to these calculations, between 1826 and 1940, around two million African slaves and around 2.5 million people from Asia arrived in the Americas.[51] Of the 2.5 million Asians that migrated across the Pacific and via the Indian and Atlantic oceans, around 1.5 million Chinese arrived mainly in the United States, Cuba, Peru, Mexico, Canada, Hawaii,

49 See the previously quoted McKeown (2008, 349-50).

50 For a good example of this, see Chang R. (2012); Gassama, Chang and Aoki (1997); Chang and Aoki (1998).

51 This does not mean that there has not been more emigration from Asia; according to Look Lai, the large majority of immigrants from China and India (7.5 and 6.3 million, respectively), they did not migrate to the Americas or to Europe during this period, but to other regions of Southern and Southeast Asia (2009, 32).

and Chile; some 600,000 Japanese arrived in Brazil, Hawaii, the United States, Canada, and Peru; and between 400,000 and 500,000 Hindu and Chinese arrived in the British, Dutch, and French colonies in the Caribbean. There was a smaller amount of Koreans, Filipinos, and other Asian and Polynesian groups that immigrated, especially to Hawaii and the United States. Some 30% of all Asian migrants during this period arrived as semi-enslaved workers or coolies, which is why it can be deduced that approximately 1.75 million Asians migrated freely (or with contracts that were less abusive in relative terms) to the Americas, as depicted in the following table:

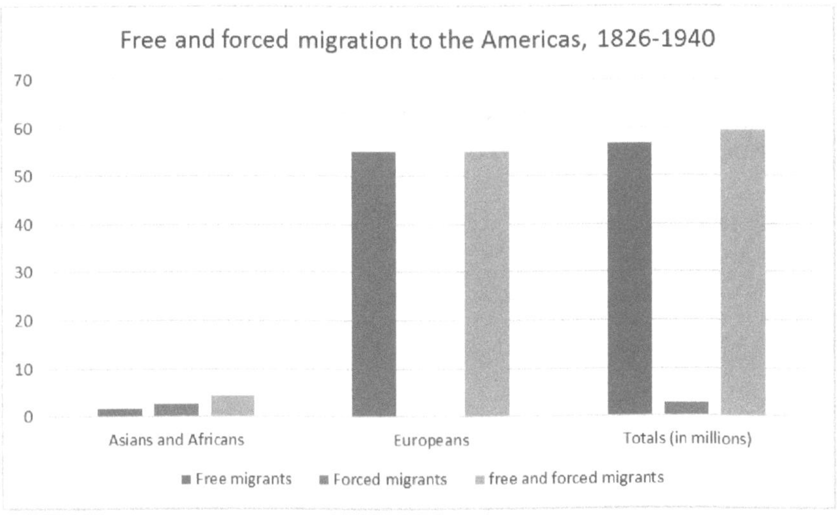

Table 2[52]

Although these numbers only represent an approximation, it can be concluded that the great free migratory movement to the Americas in the modern age before the Second World War was primarily the

52 McKeown (2004, 156); FitzGerald and Cook-Martín (2014, 36); Hu-DeHart (2007, 167); Kumar Mishra (2009, 233), Zeuske (2013, 457). Forced migrants are African slaves and Chinese and Hindu 'coolies;' Japanese contracted workers are not included in the latter category.

movement of free Europeans. The free immigration of Africans was almost entirely prohibited, and that of free Asians (which was under three percent of total free migration) was quickly restricted by mechanisms of control and exclusion that did not apply to Europeans. It is known that the industrial revolution brought technological innovations that also facilitated the increased long-distance transport, to which Lucassen and Lucassen attribute the great increase in the number of migrants after 1850 (2009, 347). However, it can be deduced from the numbers mentioned here that in the case of migration to the Americas, this increase primarily favored the mass transport of free European migrants. The following chapter will show that, as soon as non-Europeans wanted to immigrate to the Americas in larger numbers, they faced rejection, discrimination, and exclusion. The same dynamics cannot be observed in all of the cases; therefore, the example of free Chinese migration to different parts of the Americas will be analyzed.

4. Free Migration of Chinese to the United States

Although two such different historical periods do not seem comparable, perhaps it is no coincidence that the two big conjunctures of discrimination and exclusion of Chinese migrants coincided with the rise of European empires: the Iberian empires in the early modern period and the Anglo-Saxon empires in the late modern period. In 1600, when there were a maximum number of 30,000 free Chinese, or Sangleyes, in the Philippines, not only was the Spanish Empire, together with the Portuguese crown, at the height of its power and territorial expansion, it was also the period of the most extreme repression of the Sangleyes. The period of coolie trade, the quasi temporal enslavement of Chinese and Hindus in the nineteenth century, occurred during the British domination in Asia; the exclusion of Chinese in the USA began after the continental expansion had ended, during the rise of the USA as the main imperial power in the Americas and the Pacific. Here, various cases of free migration to the Americas will be described in chronological order and organized by the receiving societies.

4.1. In search of the Gold Mountain

At the end of the eighteenth century, a very small number of Chinese lived on the West Coast of continental North America. Some of them, among them artisans and sailors, settled in different parts that still belonged to New Spain and British Colombia (which later became a Canadian province) (Chang-Rodríguez 2015, 113). After the United States independence, some Cantonese also arrived in states along the Atlantic Coast. It is said that the first three people to arrive were three sailors that had been recruited in Canton to sail to Baltimore in 1785 (Lai 2004, 86). Others to arrive were mostly "merchants, sailors, and students that wanted to see and explore the foreign land that people were speaking so highly of" (Chang-Rodríguez 2015, 114), they only wanted to visit for a limited amount of time. They took a trading route that the British had established with Canton and that was used by the United States:

> After coming into contact with sailors and merchants from the United States, the Chinese became excited about the opportunities in the United States, whose main trade route with China was between Canton and New England, where the first Chinese arrived via Cape Horn [...]. (Ibid.)

Neither transcontinental railways (the Trans-Isthmic Railroad of Panama was finished in 1855 and the United States Transcontinental Railroad in 1869) nor the Panama Canal had been constructed.

On February 2, 1848, the Treaty of Guadalupe Hidalgo was signed, which would end the war between the United States and Mexico. Mexico lost more than half of its territories in the treaty, among them California, which was annexed by the United States in 1848, and incorporated as the state of California in 1850. On January 24, 1848, one week prior to the armistice, James W. Marshall discovered gold at Sutter's Mill, situated some 46 miles from Sacramento and some 130 miles from San Francisco in northeast California, which at the time still belonged to Mexico. After the discovery of gold became public at the end of that same year, it triggered the famous California Gold Rush, attracting thousands and thousands of gold-seekers from all over the globe: Mexico, Chile, Europe, Turkey, Australia, and China, among others (Sinn 2013, 1). The beginning of free Chinese migration in larger numbers to the Americas occurred during two great moments of high expectations: that of finding gold and, more generally, that of taking advantage of the economic boom in California and other parts of the country since its union with the United States, and on the Pacific coast of Canada.

The rise in migration not only changed Sacramento, which was named the state capital in 1854, but it also changed Hong Kong and San Francisco more profoundly. Between 1848 and 1852, the non-indigenous population of California increased by more than 16-fold, bringing the population count in the 1852 state census to more than 250,000 people, while the population in San Francisco grew from

500 to 36,000 (Kanazawa 2005, 781; Flynn, Frost and Latham 1999a, 12). Trade between these two port cities connected the Pacific with global trade for the first time since the decline of the Manila Galleon. Therefore, the Gold Rush in California can be interpreted as the beginning of the second Pacific century: "[…] the first Pacific century was the century of Spanish supremacy in the sixteenth and seventeenth centuries based on American silver, and the second Pacific century was brought on by California gold" (Sinn 2013, 321, note 5).

Cantonese migrants, incentivized by North American and British agents and consuls, left China with the hopes of a better life, possibly through seeking their fortune in the 'Gold Mountain' (in Cantonese *Gam Saan*, in Mandarin Jin Shan 金山). This was the name they gave California and later to the British colonies of British Columbia (now Canada) and Bendigo (state of Victoria) in Australia ('Great Mountain of Gold', Da Jin Shan 大金山),[53] where they migrated to starting in the 1850s, attracted by the same prospects. They were part of the Chinese diaspora on the West Coast of the United States and Canada, Hawaii, Australia, New Zealand, and South Africa, having been attracted by the expansion of the Anglo-Saxon colonial settlements and the economic boom (Yu 2017, 346). The vast majority of this diaspora were Chinese laborers (both coolies and free migrants) that Look Lai describes as the "global movement of Chinese unskilled manual labor (*huagong*) in this period," (2010, 2) distinguishing it from "the centuries-old movement of traders (*huashang*), artisans, and skilled workers who migrated mainly to Southeast Asia" (ibid.). Nevertheless, there was an important difference between those who migrated within the semi-slave system of coolie trade and free migrants:

> The Chinese who migrated to the United States did not come as coolies. Instead, they usually came using their own resources or under a credit-ticket system that financed their passage. Opponents

53 The name for San Francisco in Mandarin (Jiujin Shan 旧金山 [classic: 舊金山]) still originated from this meaning.

> of Chinese immigration often made no distinction between the free and semifree migration of Chinese to the United States and coerced coolies to other parts of the Americas. Labeling all Chinese immigration as a coolie migration helped to galvanize the anti-Chinese movement. (Lee 2003, 262, note 11)

In China, the name for Chinese who emigrated was *wah kiu* in Cantonese and *huaqiao* (华侨) in Mandarin ("Chinese citizen living abroad"), or *haiwai huaqiao* (海外华侨, "Overseas Chinese") (Yu 2017, 344). Kuhn explains that in Mandarin the concept of migrant itself does not indicate the direction of the migration or the permanence of the migrant abroad, so it does not specifically refer to *e*migrants, *im*migrants, or *re*migrants:

> The Chinese equivalents [to 'migrate'] are qiao 僑 (to live temporarily away from home) or yi 移 (to move, either transitive or intransitive), as in yimin 移民 (to move people, or people who move, with or without intent to remain). A narrower sense of qiao is to live abroad but keep one's Chinese nationality. (Kuhn 2008, 5, note 3)

Kuhn argues that this may be an indication that, up until that time, the majority of Chinese migrants did not intend on settling permanently outside of their country, but rather temporarily settled to work and later return to their communities. Kuhn bases this argument on the numbers provided by Sugihara Kaoru, who for the ports of Xiamen, Shantou, and Hong Kong calculated some 14.7 million emigrants from China between 1869 and 1939, and some 11.6 million people who returned in nearly the same time period (1873–1939) (ibid., 5-6, note 4).The characteristics of the mobility schemes of Chinese abroad did not seem to be permanence and separation, but the multiplicity of the forms and frequency of migration and the connection between communities. Even for those who permanently settled elsewhere, the transnational connections were a factor of fundamental importance (ibid., 4).

The majority of those who arrived in California at this stage were not traders, but rather agricultural workers and fishers from southern and southeastern China (*punti* and *hakka* like the coolies) and almost all were men. Different from the coolies, of those who freely emigrated from China to the Americas a good part belonged to the middle classes, just like other migrants that went to the Americas voluntarily. Internal migration to bigger cities in China gave way to transpacific migration "in order to accumulate additional wealth and to maintain their family's prosperity and status in China for future generations" (Lee 2003, 113). The migrants mainly came from the region of the Pearl River Delta and municipalities near the province of Canton (now Guangdong), which is now a very productive region.[54]

According to McKeown, the vast majority was even native to only seven municipalities, which is a comparatively small area where Cantonese and various Cantonese dialects, Hakka, and the Chaozhou dialect are spoken: the "four counties", *Siyi* (四邑 in Mandarin and *Sze Yap* in Cantonese) and the "three counties", *Sanyi* (三邑 in Mandarin and *Sam Yup* in Cantonese)[55]. Fifteen percent of Chinese migrants to the United States, Hawaii, and Peru were Hakka (McKeown 2001, 62-63).[56] The number of Sanyi who migrated to the United States were not as high as that of the Siyi, but they were from a more prosperous class, among them many traders, especially in the municipality of Nanhai (López 2013, 168).

They migrated for different reasons. Along with the prospect of a better future, factors that motivated people to emigrate mostly had to do with a difficult situation in the region of origin. Traditionally,

---

54 It is part of the province Canton (now Guangdong) that, with Macao and Hong Kong, is now aspiring to transform itself from one of the most productive regions in the world to one of the most innovative, following the example of San Francisco Bay and emulating the Silicon Valley model (Cyrill 2018; Preen 2019).

55 Siyi: Taishan (台山縣), Kaiping (開平縣), Enping (恩平縣) and Xinhui (新會縣); Sanyi: Nanhai (南海), Panyu (番禺) and Shunde (顺德), all in Mandarin and pinyin transcription. Municipal borders at that time are not exactly those of today, and today almost all of them are integrated into cities.

56 Lai specifies that in the case of Hawaii, 25% was Hakka and the rest were from Xiangshan (2004, 20).

over-population, land scarcity, armed conflict, and the pressures of eastern imperialism have been mentioned as contributing factors of a climate that facilitated their decision (Lee 2003, 112). Among the conflicts that shook the region were the Taiping Rebellion (1850–1864), a big civil war, and local conflicts, such as the Red Turban Rebellion (1854–1856), and the ethnic war between the *punti* and *hakka* (1856–1870) that was also felt among the emigrated communities in the Americas (Chen 1997, 525-526; Martín 1939).

Chen doubts this traditional opinion because it does not explain why people moved so far away and in such high numbers, and almost exclusively from this region. Chen maintains that the structural causes in the long and medium term and the underlying dynamics of this phenomenon must be kept in mind. In fact, they point out the fact that the Pearl River Delta at the time was a flourishing region, one of the most prosperous in China. Therefore, with respect to migration to California it was more "[…] a choice rather than a desperate flight" (Chen 1997, 522). They attribute the structural factors that facilitated emigration to the special development that Canton (the province and especially its capital that shares its name) had experienced through establishing relationships with foreign powers. That is, while they do not negate the existence of adverse conditions and great need, they opine that this was no more prevalent than in other regions of China, hence the region was able to develop key, close relationships with Western powers that later controlled all movement in the Pacific. Another important factor is the proximity to the ports of emigration and chain migration, meaning that the first to migrate were "paving the way for their fellow townsmen and villagers to follow" (ibid., 526).[57] López (2004) also analyzed this phenomenon in his research on Chinese immigrants in Cuba.

Approaching the migrants' personal reasons and self-ascription of identity is too complicated, especially for themselves. According to McKeown, this can be observed in the story of Lee K.K., a laundryman interviewed by the sociologist Paul Siu in 1930: "We over-

57 For this type of migration to the Americas see also Marquiegui (1994).

seas people can find no place in China. We can only spend money when we get back to China. No matter how much money we bring home, but as soon as the money is spent, we must come back here" (Siu as quoted in McKeown 2001, 1). McKeown argues that Siu's notion of his own transnationalized identity does not correspond with his vision because they cannot liberate themselves from the necessity of identifying themselves by their place of origin or by that of the place they have chosen to live. He describes it as

> [...] the difficulty of producing formulations of identity and history that are not centered in nation-states or other territorially based sociocultural grouping. [...] Nonetheless, such a global perspective is necessary to understand cultural and organizational aspects of Chinese migration. (Ibid.)

It can be added that this perspective is especially useful in the analysis of the interconnectedness of the Chinese diaspora in the Americas since it focuses on the networks, connections, and new hybrid identities that result from migration and the processes of transculturation.

In the above analysis of the coolie trade, we saw that the first Opium War brought the British occupation of Hong Kong, which, among other outcomes, benefitted the Anglo-Saxon control of access to the Pacific. With the discovery of gold in California, other news also came of the development of a consumer market due to the fortunes that supposedly flooded the region over night. It is said that the first to deliver this news was Chum Ming, a merchant from Canton who settled in San Francisco in 1847 and wrote a letter to his friend Cheong Yum in Canton, notifying him about the discovery of gold (Lai 2004, 86). The news immediately prompted the merchants in Hong Kong to begin transpacific trade. When the British occupied Hong Kong it was in their interest to turn its colony into a free port to serve as an *entrepôt* for British trade with China. But "nobody could have foreseen" (Sinn 2013, 43) that it would also become an *entrepôt* for the migration of thousands and thousands of people from China to California.

In 1849, 300 Chinese embarked from Hong Kong to San Francisco, the following year 450, and 2,700 in 1851, many of whom returned with gold, proving the myth a reality (although they and the maritime companies all exaggerated the possibility of striking it rich in order to promote their business) (Sinn 2013, 3). Between 1852 and 1854, the number shot through the roof: between March of 1852 and February of 1853 alone, 17,246 people on 86 ships arrived in San Francisco from Hong Kong (ibid., 314-320, Appendix 3). After the Gold Rush ended and the extraction of this precious metal was turned into an industrialized business with a paid work force (Kanazawa 2005, 782), both the number of those who traveled as well as those who stayed in California dropped considerably, continuing on from there to other regions of the Western United States. Regardless of that, other work opportunities, such as building the railways, the logging industry, fishing, agriculture, mining, and a large number of jobs in the cities (as laundrymen, in restaurants, etc.), continued to attract the Cantonese. Between 1852 and the first quarter of 1876, some 214,000 Chinese arrived in San Francisco, while some 90,000 returned to Hong Kong during the same period. This leaves a balance of some 124,000 that appear to have stayed in the United States (Sinn 2013, 312, table A2.1).[58]

The numbers are not exact, but they approximately correspond with the number of 105,465 people of Chinese origin (100,686 men and 4,779 women) who, according to the 1880 census, lived in the United States that year.[59] Among a population of around a total of 50.3 million people[60], the Chinese population formed about .2% of it, and Chinese women made up only around .1% of the population. However, the fact that they were a very small immigrant group

58 Chang speaks of some 300,000 who arrived between 1852 and 1882, and of some 200,000 who returned to China (2012, 146).

59 Calculated based on the data in the table "Population, by Sex and Race, 1790 to 1970" (U.S. Bureau of Census 1975, part 1, 14).

60 "Annual Population Estimates for the United States: 1790 to 1970" (U.S. Bureau of Census 1975, part 1, 8).

among the total number of immigrants in the United States did not protect them from the racism they were to be confronted with:

> Their small numbers notwithstanding, Chinese immigrants were the targets of racial hostility, discriminatory laws, and violence. This racism was grounded in an American Orientalist ideology that homogenized Asia as one indistinguishable entity and positioned and defined the West and the East in diametrically opposite terms, using those distinctions to claim American and Anglo-American superiority. (Lee 2003, 25)

The following will analyze how the attitudes in different phases of discrimination and exclusion of the Chinese unfolded in the United States.

4.2. The First Phase of Discrimination of Chinese Immigrants (1848–c. 1865)

Even before the start of the era of formal exclusion in 1882, there were already many different forms of discrimination against Chinese, which this chapter will focus on. From the beginning of Chinese migration to the United States at the end of the 1840s, Chinese immigrants had settled not only in San Francisco, but in various parts along the Pacific Coast and in the Western United States where they could find work. In the first decades, migration to the United States was not limited, but the access to citizenship according to the Naturalization Law of 1790 was limited to immigrants who were free 'white' people of good character:

> That any alien, being a free white person, who shall have resided within the limits and under the jurisdiction of the United States for the term of two years, may be admitted to become a citizen thereof, [...] making proof [...] that he is a person of good character [...].[61]

---

61 *1790 Naturalization Act*, Sess. II, Chap. 3; 1 stat 103. 1st Congress; March 26, 1790. The necessary period of residence in order to become a citizen was prolonged to five, and later to 14 years in 1795 and 1798, re-

This reflected the parameters with which the majority of the 'white' US-American (89% were products of British, Scottish, and Irish immigration, and almost all of the rest were German, Danish, and Swedish) Protestants (99% of the population) excluded the indigenous part of the population and those of African descent, enslaved or freed (Almaguer 1994, 23).

With the annexation of California by the United States, the "multiracial population" (De Graaf, Mulroy, and Taylor 2001, 6) that had lived there during colonial rule also had to suffer the consequences of the application of this and other laws that racialized the United States of America in a very different way. The annexation of Mexican California and subsequent massive immigration delivered a fatal blow not only to Native Americans but also to African Americans living there:

> These two events signaled the end of an era for the small population of African Americans in California. The Gold Rush rapidly "Americanized" California, and racially restrictive legislation and black slavery soon followed. (Ibid., 8)

This 'Americanization' was the product of the massive immigration of 'white' men from other parts of the United States, especially the immigration from Central and Northern Europe. While in 1850 Mexicans still made up the largest group of immigrants (especially miners from the Mexican state of Sonora), in the following years European immigrants quickly caught up, followed by the Chinese. From the 146,528 immigrants that lived in California in 1860, 45.75% were Irish (33,147), German (21,646), and British (12,227), as opposed to 34,935 Chinese (23.8%) and 9,150 Mexican (6.24%) (Almaguer 1994, 27). The indigenous peoples living in California in 1850 were not only confronted with, but decimated by the population boom of non-indigenous within a very short time, the vast majority of immigrants having been single European men. It is esti-

spectively. See *1795 Naturalization Act*, Sess. II, Chap. 19, 20; 1 stat 414. 3rd Congress; January 29, 1795 and *1798 Naturalization Act*, Sess II, Chap. 54; 1 stat 566. 5th Congress; June 17, 1798.

mated that while in 1850 some 100,000 Native Americans lived in California, in 1870 there was only about a fifth of the population left (ibid., 26, 29).

Although they did not suffer the same misfortune of Native Americans, it soon became apparent to African Americans and others who were not considered 'white' that social mobility and moving up in a colonized society and immigration was reserved for one individual group:

> […] the white "producing class." Its members alone where seen as the "value carriers" of the new social order; only they would enjoy the enormous opportunities that rapid economic development made possible. Non-white populations, on the other hand, continued to be viewed as unwelcome obstacles to the economic mobility of European Americans. (Ibid., 32)

Meaning that with the annexation of Mexican California, its "rapid transformation […] into a white masculinist preserve for European-American men found popular support in racializing ideologies" (ibid.) that were also widespread in Europe and among 'white' elites in Latin America. This "rationalized the superordinate position of the white population" (ibid.) in California and elsewhere in the United States. The ideology of the expansionist doctrine of manifest destiny that had been the foundation for westward expansion on the North American continent also served as a foundation for the legitimacy and justification of the colonization of the entire territory of the United States, which now stretches from one ocean to another.

Initially, this still did not gravely affect Chinese immigrants; they still normatively fit into the scheme of racial classification. It was not until 1870 that "Chinese difference" (Wong 2015, 4) was formally being identified "as a 'race' reclassified by the 1870 Naturalization Act" (ibid.). Furthermore, towards the end of the 1870s, the discrimination against the Chinese reached a head, and in 1882 the federal Chinese Exclusion Act was passed, defining Chinese as "aliens ineligible to citizenship" (ibid.). Nevertheless, even before the coordinated campaigns against the Chinese, there were conjunctures of discrimination and violence against them; the following will briefly look at the first phase of the conjuncture before the era of exclusion began.

It is known that this period in US-American history one of the "darkest aspects [...] is the way that certain ethnic groups were treated by the predominately white majority" (Kanazawa 2005, 779). Before the Civil War, economic development was largely based on the exploitation of enslaved Africans and the expulsion and extermination of the indigenous in the name of developing the vast territory that was incorporated through the continental expansion. According to Kanazawa, Chinese immigrants represented "a third example of how ethnic minorities were mistreated during this period" (ibid.), the only difference was that they had migrated voluntarily.[62]

Gold extraction was a business for entrepreneurs who competed bitterly for the access to the best claims: "all miners were competitive threats but foreign, and especially Chinese, miners bore the brunt of antagonism from native miners in part because it was easier to rationalize excluding them" (Kanazawa 2005, 782). Incidents of armed miners driving out foreign miners – individually or in groups – happened frequently. The first of such incidents of direct violence toward Chinese were revolts in the areas near mining activity, such as the revolt in Tuolumne in 1849 (Chen 1992, 4; Lai 2004, 88). In 1850, the state of California introduced the Foreign Miners Act that taxed foreign miners 20$ a month (an exaggeratedly large sum at the time) for the right to mine; most of these foreigners at the time were Latin Americans from Mexico and South America. Although the effect was not nearly as great as intended with the Act, some estimate that its implicit goal of driving away Mexican miners, of which a possible number of 10,000 may have been displaced by the measure. The Act was soon abrogated and in 1853 it was replaced

62 Beth Lew-Williams reminds us that historians often and wrongly minimize anti-Chinese violence by comparing its metrics to the "staggeringly lethal violence unleashed against Native Americans and African Americans" (2018, 3).

by a per capita monthly tax of 4$ for all foreign miners who gained higher yields in the state of California. Another measure aimed more directly at Chinese immigration was the commutation tax that was introduced during this same period. It required incoming ships to pay a 500$ bond for each foreign passenger, which could be exchanged for an immediate payment of between 5 and 50$ (Kanazawa 2005, 784-786). An 1854 amendment to the tax law stipulated that the tax was exclusively applicable to Chinese miners (McClain and Wu McClain 1991, 4). Taxation often became an instrument used to the detriment of Chinese immigrants.

The rejection by a large part of European American miners who wanted to get rid of the Chinese competition was joined by the political elite of the state, although there were some opposing opinions. In 1851 and early 1852 the then governor of California, John McDougal, praised Chinese immigrants as "one of the most worthy classes of our newly adopted citizens – to whom the climate and the character of these lands are peculiarly suited."[63] Only a few months later, however, his successor, Governor John Bigler, with his 'white' miner constituency in mind, lobbied for the exclusion of Chinese in the state and the Democratic Party officially approved the first anti-Chinese resolution during its convention in Benicia (Chen 1992, 4). This was a time of ups and downs for the Chinese community, whose representatives fought a legal battle so that its members could have the same rights as other immigrants who, after a certain period of residency, were able to gain citizenship.

Their representatives were the associations of Cantonese merchants in San Francisco native to the Sanyi region who protested this and other measures and published defenses that were translated from Cantonese to English for better dissemination if they were not already written in English (Lai 2004, 88). One of these was presented by Norman Asing, also known as Sang Yuen. Native to the Pearl River Delta, he had traveled from Macau to Europe and from there continued on to New York, where he decided to stay around

---

63 As cited in Barth (1964, 136). See also McClain (1994, 9).

1820. Traveling through other parts of the United States, at the beginning of the 1820s he had settled in San Francisco where he owned a restaurant. He was one of the founders of the Yeong district and a known speaker for the Chinese community. On April 25, 1852, the popular newspaper *Daily Alta California* published Asing's response to Bigler's policies. Argumentatively eloquent and clear, Asing refuted each of the governor's arguments:

> You are deeply convinced, you say, "that to enhance the prosperity and preserve the tranquility of this State, Asiatic immigration must be checked." This, your Excellency, is but one step towards a retrograde movement of the government [...]. (Asing 1852, 10)

Referring to the essence of the foundation of the United States – immigration – he reminded Bigler of his own immigrant background:

> [...] immigration made *you what you are* [sic] – and your nation what it is. [...] I am sure your Excellency cannot, if you would, prevent your being called the descendant of an immigrant, for I am sure you do not boast of being a descendant of the red man. (Ibid.)

With that he took up the racist argument of the superiority of the 'white race' and European civilization with which Bigler tried to take away Chinese immigrants' right to belong to the nation:

> But your further logic is more reprehensible. You argue that this is the republic of a particular race – that the Constitution of the United States admits of no asylum to any other than the pale face. This proposition is false in extreme, and you know it. The declaration of your independence, and all the acts of your government, your people, and your history are all against you. (Ibid.)

Here Asing referred to the equality of all immigrants in this country based on the principal of "self-evident truths" as stated in the American Declaration of Independence of 1776: "We hold these Truths to be self-evident, that all Men are created equal [...]" (*U.S. Declaration of Independence*). Asing even argued that, besides the obvious physiognomic differences, it is not fair to establish a hierarchy or inequality between the human 'races':

> As far as regards the color and complexion of our race, we are perfectly aware that our population have [sic] been a little more tanned than yours. Your Excellency will discover, however, that we are as much allied to the *African* race and the red man as you are yourself, and that as far as the aristocracy of *skin* is concerned, ours might compare with many of the European races; nor do we consider that your Excellency, as a Democrat, will make us believe that the framers of your declaration of rights ever suggested the propriety of establishing an aristocracy of *skin*. (Asing 1852, 11)[64]

He also points out that the superiority of Chinese culture has been noted and respected by many European scholars and educated people, which made Bigler's arguments of the European cultural, morals, and racial superiority seem even more mistaken.

There were also European Americans who defended the Chinese community, including the Presbyterian reverend William Speer who had been in Canton as a missionary. In 1852, the Presbyterian Board of Foreign Mission sent him to California to continue his missionary work with Chinese immigrants (Stahler 1970, 114), who were considered 'pagans,' an epithet frequently used by the Californian press to degrade them and brand them as different. In contrast to the situation in China, in California missionaries had the support of the government and a society obsessed with religious conversion to the prevalent religion. L. Ling-Chi Wang interpreted it as follows: "In fact, American desire to convert the heathen Chinese was a national obsession" (2008).

Speer spoke fluent Cantonese and quickly became a trusted person among the Chinese community in San Francisco. While he hoped the Christianized Chinese would return to their place of origin in order to multiply and therefore increase the number of people practicing the religion, he was troubled by the growing aversion the Chinese in California had to endure. In 1855, the newspaper

64 Italics in the original.

Oriental (*Tung-ngai san-luk*) began being published in a Cantonese edition (daily) and a bilingual edition (three times a week). Besides its religious mission, this newspaper advocated for the reversal of the legislation that discriminated against the Chinese. Thanks to this and other pressures, the 1855 taxation law was reversed and the monthly poll tax was reduced to 4$ a month (McClain 1994, 19-20).

The protests of Asing and other representatives of the Chinese community who advocated for them, such as Speer, were temporarily successful, especially due to the state's dire economic situation; the taxes Chinese paid, in comparison with the state's negligible expenses for public services, such as education and health care, were vital to the operation and development of California in those early years (Kanazawa 2005, 781). Even so, at both the local and state level legislation was being passed that was aimed to exclude the Chinese. For example, in 1854, the Chinese community experienced a major setback with the Supreme Court of California's decision that no Chinese person was able to serve as a witness in a trial against a 'white' person. In the now sadly renowned case of People v. Hall, Supreme Court of California deliberated on the case of George W. Hall, who appealed the guilty verdict for the murder of the miner Ling Sing. The witnesses, just like the victim, were of Chinese origin. In its decision, Judge Hugh C. Murray followed the argumentation of the Hall's lawyers and made the decision that disqualified all Chinese as witnesses in the court of law. Hall was acquitted and the murder went unpunished.

This case is still significant today because it easily transcended a case between two individuals, regardless of the seriousness of the crime. What was Murray's argumentation and what were the implications? The sentence racialized the implicated individuals, amplifying the pre-existing distinctions between 'white' and 'non-white' people from the Chinese. Indigenous and African Americans had already been excluded from participating in society as citizens, having been denied various human rights, exposed to discrimination, exclusion, and severe exploitation. This last one was reflected in both civil and criminal law, which stipulated:

> No black or mulatto person, or Indian, shall be permitted to give evidence in favor of, or against, any white person. Every person who shall have one eighth part or more of Negro [sic] blood shall be deemed a mulatto, and every person who shall have one half of Indian blood shall be deemed an Indian.[65]

Up until that moment, Chinese had not been formally excluded from the US-American society, but now the Supreme Court of California assigned them the same status as the indigenous and African Americans, who did not have the right to citizenship. In his sentencing, Judge Murray argued: "*Held*, that the words, Indian, Negro [sic], Black and White, are generic terms, designating race. That, therefore, Chinese and all other people not white, are included in the prohibition from being witnesses against Whites,"[66] to which he later added the category "mulatto" (ibid.). With that he contributed significantly to the implementation of racist conception in the law and established a precedence of inequality that would influence future decisions about the ethnic status of all the inhabitants of California and beyond. To argue the inclusion of the Chinese in the group of excluded peoples, Murray expanded in length (referring back to the arrival of Christopher Columbus in the Americas and his invention of the 'Indian') to reach the conclusion that both the indigenous of the Americas as well as the peoples of Asia and the Pacific belonged to the same 'race' – the "Mongolian, or Asiatic" (ibid.). Furthermore, he explicitly established a norm that openly degraded non-European immigrants as a way of trying to avoid "anomalous consequences" (ibid.) with this sentence:

> The European white man who comes here would not be shielded from the testimony of the degraded and demoralized caste, while the Negro [sic], fresh from the coast of Africa, or the Indian of Pat-

---

65 "An Act concerning Crimes and Punishments", in: California State Assembly: *Statutes and Amendments to the Codes 1850*, Statute 99 §14, p. 230.

66 Supreme Court of California: "THE PEOPLE, Respondent, v. GEORGE W. HALL, Appellant. Cal. 1854." In the following *People v. Hall.*

> agonia, the Kanaka, South Sea Islander, or New Hollander, would be admitted, upon their arrival, to testify against white citizens in our courts of law. To argue such a proposition would be an insult to the good sense of the Legislature" (ibid.).

Referring to the initial argument of the Federal Naturalization Law (originally of 1790), Murray again emphasized the exceptionality and superiority of the white 'race' that distinguished it from all other 'races:' "The word 'White' has a distinct signification, which *ex vi termini*, excludes black, yellow, and all other colors" (ibid.). He tried to form his creation of 'whiteness' both through the idea of exceptionalism and singularity of the 'white race,' and through the glorification of 'the white' based on bioethical markers. According to Murray, the negation of the equality of people is a logical consequence of the natural differences between human beings according to their physical characteristics and their character. With that he wanted to discursively rid himself of any responsibility for his racist decision, searching for resources and excuses in natural forces that are out of his reach. In order to further strengthen his argument, he described the potential consequences of a supposed equality between 'races,' specifically between the inhabitants of California of European decent and those of Chinese decent as a type of threat:

> The same rule which would admit them to testify, would admit them to all the equal rights of citizenship, and we might soon see them at the polls, in the jury box, upon the bench, and in our legislative halls.
>
> This is not a speculation which exists in the excited and overheated imagination of the patriot and statesman, but it is an actual and present danger.
>
> The anomalous spectacle of a distinct people, living in our community, recognizing no laws of this State except through necessity, bringing with them their prejudices and national feuds, in which they indulge in open violation of law; whose mendacity is proverbial; a race of people whom nature has marked as inferior, and who are incapable of progress or intellectual development beyond a certain point, as their history has shown; differing in language, opin-

> ions, color, and physical conformation; between whom and ourselves nature has placed an impassable difference, is now presented, and for them is claimed, not only the right to swear away the life of a citizen, but the further privilege of participating with us in administering the affairs of our Government." (*People v. Hall*)

It is interesting that a judge such as Murray would argue in such a manner, for his character seems to have been diametrically opposed to the ethical values he expected of the Chinese, as Hubert Howe Bancroft described years later:

> Probably the most notorious of all our supreme judges was Hugh C. Murray, a man utterly abandoned in character, immoral, venal, and thoroughly corrupt. Even in those days of unblushing laxity he was prominent for impudent indecorum. Among gamblers he was always at home [...]; of drinking saloons he was a constant habitué [...]. Shoulder-strikers were his friends, lewd women his companions; he was a Californian Caligula, with his adherent politicians, gladiators, and courtesans. [...] And what made it the worse for the country was that from his decisions there was no appeal – only from Hugh Murray drunk to Hugh Murray sober. (Bancroft 1888, 605-606)

The reactions to *People v. Hall* among the Chinese community in San Francisco were immediate. In 1855, the well-known merchant Lai Chun-chuen attacked Murray's decision in an open letter to governor Bigler. He also relied on racist arguments in his argumentation: scandalizing the equalization of the Chinese to the indigenous and Africans, he argued from a perspective of cultural superiority of Chinese civilization. Referring to the supposed inferiority of the indigenous in contrast to Chinese and European civilization, he ultimately pleaded for the equality of people of Chinese and European origin (McClain 1994, 22). According to McClain, not only merchants, but Chinese from all classes resented the *People v. Hall* verdict that made them vulnerable to gross impunity and which deterred them from reporting crimes committed against them. The above mentioned Presbyterian Speer had served as an interpreter when Hall was sentenced to death by hanging in 1853, and he was stunned when he saw that the sentence had been turned over by the Supreme Court of California in *People v. Hall*, exclaiming that "[…] Republicanism, Christianity, and common humanity are all outraged by this iniquitous decision of the Supreme Court of California" (ibid.).[67]

This stance led Speer to publish a letter of protest in his book *The Oldest and the Newest Empire: China and the United States.*[68] The letter was written by a young merchant by the name of Pun Chi and translated from Cantonese into English by Speer; Pun Chi had been a student in Speer's missionary school in San Francisco in the 1850s (Speer 1870, 584). Written around 1860, at the dawn of the American Civil War and directed toward the United States Congress in Washington, Pun Chi's seventeen-page protest elaborated on the difficulties and dangers that the Chinese in California faced due to xenophobic and racist hatred. In his twelfth and last paragraph, the author summarized the great contradiction between the incentives the United States government had offered to the Chinese to immigrate and the disrespectful treatment and violence that they had to deal with:

> When we were first favored with the invitations of your ship-captains to emigrate to California, and heard the laudations which they published of the perfect and admirable character of your institutions, and were told of your exceeding respect and love toward the Chinese, we could hardly have calculated that we would now be the objects of your excessive hatred — that your courts would refuse us the right of testimony; your legislature load us with increasing taxes and devise means how to wholly expel us; that foreign villains, witnessing your degrading treatment of us, would assume the right to harass, plunder and rob us, possibly kill us […]. (Ibid., 602)

67 Quote from the "Chinese Testimony", *Oriental*, January 18, 1855, p. 3, col. 1.

68 Pun Chi: "A Remonstrance from the Chinese in California to the Congress of the United States", in: Speer (1870, 588-604).

He proposed two solutions to the congress to resolve this dilemma: the first would be to decree the complete deportation of the Chinese from the United States, for which he asked for a time frame of three years in order for everyone to have enough time to organize their affairs to return to their country of origin. The second solution would be to formally accept that the Chinese would stay and work in the United States, which would have to be accompanied by provisions of participation and legal protection and the end of "incessant discussions about the deportation of the Chinese" (ibid., 603). This study will later show that the congress did not order either one of these solutions, but instead decreed various laws that – although they did not expulse the Chinese – would seriously limit the opportunities of participation and immigration, especially for Chinese laborers.

In his analysis of the case of *People v. Hall*, Chin observed that up until that point there had not been any mention of the Chinese in the cited law[69], which is why "[…] this statute would seem inapplicable to Asians […]" (Chin 2013, 967). But when the Supreme Court of California included them in the group that couldn't testify it exposed them to every kind of crime that would go unpunished provided there was no 'white' witness. With that, impunity was extensive and crimes against the indigenous, African Americans, and mestizos of both groups was extended to anyone not considered 'white' by law. The argument to include the Chinese in this group of excluded peoples had repercussions in 1863 when "Mongolian or Chinese" (ibid., 968) was added to the paragraph of this penal code. At the same time, in 1863 African Americans were not included in this paragraph, which is why they could serve as witnesses. Chin interpreted this as a consequence of the American Civil War that would bring the abolition of slavery and the Fourteenth Amendment that granted African Americans civil and citizenship rights. However, this gradual extension of civil rights for African Americans at

69 "An Act concerning Crimes and Punishments." In California State Assembly: *Statutes and Amendments to the Codes 1850*, Statute 99 §14.

that time did not extend to the Chinese or any other Asian groups until the passing of the federal Voting Rights Act in 1870 (ibid., 968-970).

Carlin argues that the tradition that People vs. Hall started in 1854 of devaluating the testimony of a 'non-white' person in all or almost all 'white' tribunals still persists (2016, 454), just as the creation of 'whiteness' manifests in this case: "Through cases like Hall, whiteness was characterized as an exclusive category" (ibid., 457). Carlin uses this case to illustrate the unfortunately long tradition of racist exclusion that contributed to the absolution of George Zimmerman in the murder of Trayvon Martin in 2013. He attributes this impunity to the devaluation of the testimony of the key witness, Rachel Jeantel, of Haitian and Dominican descent.

Returning to the conjunctures of exclusion in the 1850s, there are also local and state laws that aimed to limit Chinese immigration and presence. In 1855, the state started directly limiting Chinese immigration by passing the "Act to Discourage the Immigration to this State of Persons who cannot become Citizens thereof" that demanded docking ships to pay a tax of 50$ for all of the people "incompetent… to become citizens" (Kanazawa 2005, 787).[70] In 1856, in the town of Tuolumne they explicitly prohibited miners from the 'South Sea' (by which they meant Oceania) to work in Tuolumne's district of Columbia. In other districts it was prohibited to buy or possess mining claims, sometimes requiring that only those who had the intention of becoming citizens could purchase them, interpreting the federal Law of Naturalization that limited the access to citizenship to "free white men," (ibid., 783) to the detriment of the Chinese.

It has been shown that both at the state and local level many European Americans of California wanted to significantly reduce Chinese immigration and even displace and exclude Chinese immigrants. In many cases, Chinese were assaulted, fleeced, and killed,

70 Quote from "An Act to Discourage the Immigration to this State of Persons who cannot become Citizens thereof," Chapter 153, *Statutes and Amendments to the Codes 1855*, pp. 194–95.

while the victimizers often went unpunished. The federal Law of Naturalization that, since 1790, reserved the right to citizenship for 'free white men' was interpreted in such a manner that Chinese were not considered part of that category, creating a legal framework to reflect the supposed superiority of the 'white race.' For that reason, fifteen years before the federal law categorized them as 'non-white,' they had already been racialized in this manner and they were denied access to citizenship in the state of California (Kanazawa 2005, 781; 787).

Although the many attempts at exclusion were successful to a certain degree in removing Chinese miners from the best gold claims, demographically they were not successful, neither before nor after the economic consolidation of California. This was mostly due to the scarcity of labor that caused a great demand for Chinese labor by the rest of the Californian society even after the Gold Rush: While they only represented less than 10% of the population in the state, they contributed 25% of the labor force that was physically able to carry out the work needed in the development of Western North America (Lai 2004, 19). The industrial ambitions that were growing with the economic boom and the building of the Transcontinental Railroad were too great to go without the labor force that the Chinese could offer. As it has been observed, neither legal mechanisms nor institutions to exclude the Chinese for ethnic reasons had yet been formally established at the federal level. At the local and state levels, however, formal and informal mechanisms were being established that were building the xenophobic foundation of what would turn the Chinese into the first objects of hatred against 'non-white' immigrants in the country.

The building of the Transcontinental Railroad acted as a kind of intermission within the dynamics of even more sever exclusion. A few months after the Civil War broke out, the new governor of California, Leland Stanford, was prepared not only to continue racist policies against Chinese living in the state, but to take it to extremes. In his inaugural address on January 10, 1862, Stanford (the founder of the Ivy League university that still carries his name) announced his position and plan.

> While the settlement of our State is of the first importance, the character of those who shall become settlers is worthy of scarcely less consideration. To my mind it is clear, that the settlement among us of an inferior race is to be discouraged, by every legitimate means. Asia, with her numberless millions, sends to our shores the dregs of her population. Large numbers of this class are already here [...]. There can be no doubt that the presence of numbers among us of a degraded and distinct people must exercise a deleterious influence upon the superior race, and, to a certain extent, repel desirable immigration. It will afford me great pleasure to concur with the Legislature in any constitutional action, having for its object the repression of the immigration of the Asiatic races. (*Leland Stanford Inaugural Address*)

Weeks later, the legislature established a board of three senators and three member of the assembly in order to confer with representatives of the merchant class of Chinese in California to talk about the possibilities of allowing permanent settlement for the Chinese in the state. The tone of their report was markedly in favor of Chinese immigration, which, against the background of the growing racism against Chinese at the time "seems almost a historical anomaly" (McClain 1994, 25). According to McClain, this was the last report of the nineteenth century from a California state entity that spoke positively about Californian Chinese. It praised the Chinese for being "peaceable, patient, and industrious" (ibid., 26) and highlighted the fact that they significantly contributed to the development of the state with their vocational abilities and the taxes they paid. It continues by adding that there were no indications that they took jobs from 'Caucasian' workers (ibid.), concluding that – due to the multiple restrictions that had been placed on them – they were not a threat.

Nevertheless, the report did not stop the governor from signing a law in April of 1862 that had been approved by both legislative chambers under the title "An Act to protect Free White Labor against competition with Chinese Coolie Labor and to discourage the Immigration of the Chinese into the State of California."[71] The instrument that institutionalized this law was a capitation tax called the "Chinese Police Tax" (ibid.), which was exclusively applied to adults of "the Mongolian race" (ibid.). The Chinese merchants reacted immediately, and the law was overturned through the legal case *Lin Sing v. Washburn* on the grounds that the regulation of non-domestic trade regulation was not under the jurisdiction of the state of California, but under national jurisdiction (McClain 1994, 27-29).

4.3. Building the Transcontinental Railroad and a Time of Hope during the Reconstruction Era

Gordon H. Chang, one of the directors of *Chinese Railroad Workers in North America Project* at the University of Stanford, which ended in 2019, quested why, from the very beginning of Chinese immigration to the United States (and the immediate discrimination of them), three decades passed before the passing of the federal Chinese Exclusion Act in 1882 (Chang G. 2012, 146). In line with what has been stated above, Chang arguments that regardless of the multiple attempts of exclusion, especially in the Western United States, the importance of Pacific trade, in particular with the Empire of China, was a key element of the progress of the nation:

> Access to China, and Pacific commerce more generally, free Chinese immigration, and America's future welfare formed one integrated vision in the minds of important Americans – business, political, and religious leaders among them – through much of the nineteenth century. This vision inspired their powerful opposition to immigration restriction and frustrated exclusionists until altered national and international diplomatic landscapes created the conditions for successful exclusion. (Ibid., 147)

In line with McCain's meticulous analysis, we believe, however, that the exclusion cannot be considered a failure prior to 1882 and a

71 California State Assembly, Office of the Chief Clerk: *Statutes and Amendments to the Codes 1862*, Ch. 339, 1862 Cal. Stat. 462.

success thereafter. Rather, we see that there were powerful and variable dynamics and conjunctures of exclusion that limited California and the surrounding regions with their highs and lows and more or less successful processes of negotiation during the first period, and in the second period extended to a national level for various reasons, which will be discussed below. We can observe that there was a period of hope that approximately coincided with the Reconstruction Era (1865–1877). Going back to the 1860s, we see that in the case of Lin Sing v. Washburn in 1862 was a significant victory for the Californian Chinese community by proving the unconstitutionality of the racist law of the Chinese Police Tax (Baxter 2008, 32). Apart from the Chinese community's resistance, the need for their man power during the heyday of the building of the Transcontinental Railroad seems to have brought a new, unexpected change in attitude of even the most racist and stubborn politicians in California. In a footnote, McClain cautiously proposed that this may have been the case:

> The renewed Caucasian interest in Chinese grievances might have had some connection with the new importance the Chinese were coming to assume in the state's economy. In early 1865 Charles Crocker and Leland Stanford of the Central Pacific Railway [sic], eager to push ahead with the western arm of the Transcontinental Railroad and unable to secure an adequate, reliable white labor force, decided to experiment with a small crew of Chinese laborers. The experiment was an enormous success, and within a year several thousand Chinese, many of them ex-miners now looking for more remunerative work in other sectors of the economy, were toiling away in the employ of the railroad on the western slopes of the Sierra Nevada. (McClain 1994, 298, note 163)

Stanford and Crocker were part of the Big Four, along with Collis Potter Huntington and Mark Hopkins, the owners of Central Pacific Railroad who expected enormous profits with this project of such great importance for the Union and the development of the country. The construction of the first transcontinental railroad to northern Panama had begun in 1864, but its progress left much to be desired, especially when the work approached the more dangerous and inhospitable region of the Sierra Nevada in California. Crocker tried to convince Stanford and the rest of how useful the Chinese workers would be, arguing that "[…] the race that built the Great Wall of China could certainly be useful in building a railroad [...]" (Kraus 1969, 43). The scarcity of man power at the end of the Civil War, which was also the result of the liberation of African slaves, finally managed to convince those who up until that point had maintained an openly racist and exclusionary attitude toward the Chinese.

The sociopolitical climate was favorable: On February 19, 1862, President Abraham Lincoln signed the "Act to Prohibit the 'Coolie Trade' by American Citizens in American Vessels." The law prohibited anyone living in the United States territory from participating in the coolie trade. Originally designed to avoid Chinese immigration in the context of this regime of semi-slavery, it is also considered the first law that regulated free immigration, imposing the first migratory restrictions by the United States on one single group – the Chinese:

> The law was, in another sense, the first federal statute to restrict immigration into the United States. Chinese migrants henceforth would have to prove to U.S. consuls that they were "free and voluntary" immigrants – and not coolies [...]. (Jung 2006, 37)

With the abolition of slavery through the Emancipation Proclamation of 1863, "that fundamentally changed the character of the Civil War by linking it with slavery" (Wong 2015, 23), and the 13th Amendment in 1865, all African Americans were finally formally liberated and were able to choose where they wanted to work. Furthermore, the 14th Amendment of 1868 guaranteed all people born in the United States, or those who had been naturalized, access to fundamental civil liberties, equality before the law, and equal protection by national law; for example, through the Naturalization Act of 1870.[72] However, at the time, these rights did not apply to the Chinese.

72 It is known that the discrimination of the African Americans part of the United States population once again intensified after the end of the Re-

Nevertheless, only months after Lincoln declared the abolition of the enslavement of Africans, in 1865, Stanford, who had been promoting the exclusion of Chinese migration on the basis of a supposed 'racial inferiority' during his term as governor (1862–1863), completely changed his tone. In a report to President Andrew Johnson, who succeeded Lincoln after he was assassinated, Stanford praised those who he had called "dregs" (*Leland Stanford Inaugural Address*) only three years before, using the same language of the commissioned report that he himself had rejected in 1862:

> As a class they are quiet, peaceable, patient, industrious and economical. Ready and apt to learn all the different kinds of work required in railroad building, they soon become as efficient as white laborers. More prudent and economical, they are contented with less wages. (Kraus 1969, 45)[73]

In contrast, many European American workers were unwilling to do such hard work for comparatively little pay: "A large majority of the white laboring class on the Pacific Coast find more profitable and congenial employment in mining and agricultural pursuits, than in railroad work" (ibid., 47). And there is no doubt that the (at its peak) more than 15,000 Chinese workers were diligent ones: not only did they build the most difficult and dangerous part of the train tracks, but they did it in record time, maximizing the productivity and speed of the work on the last stretch: On the day of April 28, 1869, they built a total of ten miles of railroad tracks and beat the record set by their Irish (and other European American) contemporaries

---

construction Era, especially with the lynching done by the Ku Klux Klan and the racial segregation laws of the Jim Crow era, which, regardless of the great achievements of the civil rights movement of the 1950s and 1960s, still exist today.

73 Quoted by Erie Heath, "From Trail to Rail," *Southern Pacific Bulletin*, XV (1927), Chap. XV, p. 12. Chinese merchants and intermediaries from San Francisco participated in the recruitment and organization of the working teams, guaranteeing the reliable and constant flow of workers and maintaining social control by way of association based on clans, origin, and more (ibid.).

that came from the eastern part of the country with the Union Pacific Railroad Company. Days later, the teams found themselves in the territory of Utah, completing one of the greatest works of the nineteenth century. Nevertheless, when Stanford drove the last spike (made of gold) into the railroad on May 10, 1869 during the Promontory Summit ceremony in Utah, not even one of the Chinese workers present at the occasion appeared in the official photograph of the 'Golden Spike' ceremony. The picture, which apparently also shows no African Americans, Native Americans or women, sends the message that the Union and progress of the country was being achieved by "free white labor" for "free white men."

Detail from *East and West Shaking Hands at Laying Last Rail*, 1869, photograph by Andrew J. Russel. Public Domain.[74]

74 https://upload.wikimedia.org/wikipedia/commons/5/5d/East_and_West_Shaking_hands_at_the_laying_of_last_rail_Union_Pacific_Railroad_-_Restoration.jpg.

The absence of the Chinese could be interpreted as an omen of what was to come after having successfully completed their arduous job of contributing so significantly to the building of the railway tracks that was to connect the Pacific Coast region with the rest of the country: we don't need you now, you may go. As Kraus concludes:

> With the completion of the Central Pacific, many Chinese workers moved to other railroad construction jobs, including some for the Central Pacific. Others returned with their savings to their families in Canton. Others still sent to China for wives and settled in various western communities as laundrymen and restaurateurs. The majority who remained, however, returned to the Pacific Coast. (1969, 57)

Kraus, careful not to shad the 150th anniversary of the event in this commemorative publication, omitted the repression that many of them suffered after having finished their work on the railroad and the period of exclusion that awaited those to come.

However, at no point in time had racist attitudes or discourse completely dissipated, and people were still propagating apocalyptic pictures of the future of the 'white race' at the hands of Chinese and Irish immigration. Both groups had been systematically degraded since setting foot in the United States and were seen as a threat to Protestant European Americans. In cartoons, the Irish were frequently portrayed as having African features to differentiate them from other, supposedly superior Europeans.[75] This comes as no surprise as the construct of 'whiteness' was not only based on factors derived from the physical appearance of individuals (the supposed 'race'), it was identifiable through one's behavior, values, language, religion, social position, and power, which Barkan considers to be a fundamental aspect of the construction of a white identity (2007, 9).

---

75 See, for example, the caricature "Irish, Anglo-Teutonic, and Negro [sic] heads," in H. Strickland Constable, *Ireland from One or Two Neglected Points of View*, 1899, quoted and depicted in Bornstein (2014, 146). It used the basis of scientific racism to help explain that the origin of an "Irish Iberian" was closer to that of Africans than to that of the "Anglo-Teutonic."

The Irish were not only distinguished from the 'white' US-Americans because of their Catholic faith, but people also questioned their "'racial' status as whites" (ibid., 8) because many of them were poor and illiterate. Something similar would happen to other immigrant groups in the coming decades, the 'white' status of which the European Americans of Anglo-Saxon origin also questioned.[76]

Lithograph. San Francisco, c. 1869. Courtesy of the Library of Congress.[77]

76 For example, Southern and Eastern European immigrants from the late nineteenth century until the 1920s (Barrett and Roediger 2002, 29).

77 "The Great Fear of the Period: That Uncle Sam may be swallowed by foreigners. The problem solved." San Francisco: White & Bauer, [be-

In the first two images in this caricature, US-Americans represented by Uncle Sam are being devoured by an Irish and a Chinese man, representing the respective immigrant groups. They are standing on top of a map of the United States that stretches from the Atlantic to the Pacific Ocean as seen from the northern border; the Gulf of Mexico is in the background. The geography shows details, such as the railroad tracks with steam engines to symbolize the progress of the construction of the Transcontinental Railroad. This project, which was not only going to connect the Atlantic and Pacific regions but the entire nation, was used here as a symbol for the destruction of the nation by groups of undesirable immigrants. This xenophobic image perverts the railroad worker's efforts, silencing their exploitation by the elite European Americans, appealing here to the attitudes held by the California reading public and reinforcing them. The culminating point is shown in the third image as the Chinese immigrant ends up devouring the Irish immigrant, reflecting the extent of racist attitudes that propagated the possible disappearance of all of the 'whites' if the state kept opening its door to Asian immigration. The caricature's cannibalistic metaphor can be seen in the context of a long tradition of descriptions of the 'other' in the Americas as dangerous and savage, dehumanizing anyone of non-European descent.

Apart from the continued racist attitudes, it can be ascertained that the second half of the 1860s was an exceptional phase of temporarily relaxed tensions during which the vision of a future of the coexistence between people of Asian and European descent seemed possible. This feeling was fed by an extraordinary rapprochement between the United States government and that of the Empire of China. The Burlingame Treaty of 1868 was the result of the first diplomatic visit by the Qing government to the United States. Substantially modifying the Treaty of Tianjin of 1858, it was the first treaty that respected the rights of both parties as equals since the

---

tween 1860 and 1869]. Library of Congress Prints and Photographs Division.

humiliating treaties between China and European powers that resulted from the Opium Wars (Schrecker 2010, 9).

This was a big step in the direction of mutual respect between both countries, including the immigrants and residents of each nation residing in the other. Although the treaty did not explicitly regulate the right of naturalization in the country of destination, article 5 holds the right of free and voluntary migration between both nations and, while banning forced migration – clearly alluding to coolie trade that was still being practiced to supply the British and Spanish colonies and countries such as Peru with a semi-enslaved work force (Burlingame Treaty 1868, 4). It permitted people to move between both countries for pretty much any reason: "[...] for the purpose of curiosity, of trade, or as permanent residents" (ibid.). Furthermore, travelers from both countries were guaranteed freedom of religion in its article 4, and access to public education in article 7. The pinnacle of the treaty, article 6, grants both Chinese travelers and residents in the United States the same protection that US-Americans had in China. The article in its entirety said:

> Citizens of the United States visiting or residing in China shall enjoy the same privileges, immunities or exemptions in respect to travel or residence as may there be enjoyed by the citizens or subjects of the most favored nation, and, reciprocally, Chinese subjects visiting or residing in the United States shall enjoy the same privileges, immunities and exemptions in respect to travel or residence as may be enjoyed by the citizens or subjects of the most favored nation. But nothing herein contained shall be held to confer naturalization upon the citizens of the United States in China, nor upon the subjects of China in the United States. (Ibid.)

Only days after having been presented to the US-American public, writer Mark Twain analyzed the treaty in his 1868 article "The Treaty with China" (Zehr 2010, 2). In his analysis of article 5, he clearly saw the condemnation of the coolie trade on par with the considerable increase of free Chinese immigration to the United States. Regardless of making it clear that he personally did not like the Chinese in the United States, he praised them:

> The present Chinese immigration, however, is the best class of people – in some respects, though not in all – that comes to us from foreign lands. They are the best railroad hands we have by far. They are the most faithful, the most temperate, the most peaceable, the most industrious. (Twain 2010)

With that he also implicitly differentiated them from the Irish immigrants, of whom Twain was very contemptuous (Ou 2009, 2). Twain paid close attention to article 6, which he awarded extraordinary potential. He argued that with this article, the treaty annulled all "intolerant and unconstitutional" (Twain 2010) laws of California against Chinese immigrants, and predicted that this was going to cause problems for the state's elite, that they were going to moan and complain. Discriminatory laws that had created a sort of Apartheid in San Francisco were now going to grant the Chinese in California equality from the personal to the highest level. They were going to be able to sit next to other passengers in the street cars, serve as witnesses against or in the favor of European Americans in court, and in the near future they would be able to become citizens due to the years of residence, which would allow them to participate in elections and even qualify them to become judges. He predicted that the European American political candidates were going to have to win over Chinese immigrants in the elections just like the German and Irish immigrants with inclusive slogans such as "THE COUNTRY'S HOPE, THE PEOPLE'S CHOICE — DONNERWETTER, O'SHAUGHNESSY, AND CHING-FOO!"[78]

Although Twain clearly realized that article 6 also maintained that they would not be granted the right to naturalization, the formulation "of the most favored nation" meant to him that it granted them the status of equals on the basis of nationality, leaving behind the inequality based on ethnic parameters. With article 7, the treaty that was well negotiated by Anson Burlingame, according to the paternalistic vision of Twain, "[...] lifts a degraded, snubbed, vilified, and hated race of men out of the mud and invests them with the

---

78 Ibid., capital letters in the original.

purple of American sovereignty. It makes men out of beasts of burden" (ibid.). And he continues: "The first iniquity it strikes at is that same revolutionary one of taxation without representation" (ibid.). Finally, an interesting aspect of Twain's article is his reflection on the development of his own xenophobia and racism toward a more tolerant attitude:

> The idea of making negroes [sic] citizens of the United States was startling and disagreeable to me, but I have become reconciled to it; and being reconciled to it, and the ice being broken and the principle established, I am now ready for all comers. The idea of seeing a Chinaman a citizen of the United States would have been almost appalling to me a few years ago, but I suppose I can live through it now. (Ibid.)

Maybe this mental development reflects that of many European Americans who were originally opposed to the Chinese for racist reasons, but then apparently began accepting a certain level of equality, always maintaining a paternalistic attitude. In the following years, Twain continued to defend the Chinese as equals under the law and accusing the police of permitting acts of violence against them; for example, in the three satiric pieces *Disgraceful Persecution of a Boy*, *John Chinaman in New York*, and *Goldsmith's Friend Abroad Again*, which were published in the magazine *The Galaxy* in 1870 and 1871 (Ou 2009, 1-8). However, the spirit of the Burlingame Treaty would not last much longer than the end of the Reconstruction Era.

4.4. The 1870s: A Time of Change

As already observed, thousands of Chinese worked for Stanford and his partners at the Central Pacific Railroad building the Transcontinental Railroad, and because there was not enough manpower in California, thousands of workers had been directly recruited in China. When the construction was finished in 1869, some were able to work on new railroad projects, for which they were transferred to states to the east of the Mississippi River, and to the South, where the labor force was beginning to thin out due to the emancipation of enslaved Africans (Lau-Fong and Lai 1992, 46).

But the vast majority of the Chinese remained unemployed. Along with the recession in those years, which left many European Americans without work, new racist and xenophobic resentment against Asians began to grow, particularly in California. In the late 1860s, the Chinese population was concentrated in San Francisco, and the 12,000 Chinese who lived there in 1870 represented approximately a quarter of the entire Chinese population in California. This was due to the decline in employment opportunities in the railroad and mining sectors, and to the rapid growth of the city as a commercial and manufacturing hub (McClain 1994, 43). According to McClain, the European-American population (or 'Caucasians'), and especially the workers,

> […] saw the Chinese not only as an alien and distasteful race but as economic competitors. The hostility manifested itself in a number of ways. One was sheer physical violence. [...] Another form of hostility was the development of organized mass opposition to the Chinese and the agitation for anti-Chinese legislation at the local level. (Ibid., 44)

The anti-Chinese movement contributed significantly to hindering Chinese people's access to the labor market: "Jobs and money were limited [...] by restrictions placed on Chinese by the anti-Chinese movement, which sought successfully to limit severely the economic opportunities available to Chinese" (Armentrout Ma 1991, 155). This resulted in growing tensions within the Chinese community that sparked internal conflicts called the "tong wars" (ibid.) because of the key role of Chinese secret societies. Moreover, the increased presence of young, unemployed Chinese workers contributed to the rise in the scarcity of living space and to a decline in sanitary conditions, while illegal gambling, opium consumption, and prostitution increased. The authorities, far from granting them access to public health, education, or the labor market, watched as the situation in

Chinatown deteriorated. A report following the inspection of Chinatown that was ordered by the San Francisco Board of Supervisors in 1885 described the state of the quarter as follows:

> [T]he general aspect of the streets and habitations was filthy in the extreme, and so long as they remained in that condition, so long would they stand as a constant menace to the welfare of society as a slumbering pest [...]. [...] it constitutes a continued source of danger of this character, and probably always will, so long as it is inhabited by people of the Mongolian race. ("Report of Special Committee on the Condition of the Chinese Quarter, and the Chinese in San Francisco" 1885, 165)

Along with alleging that the cause of the deplorable situation was due to the character of the Chinese, they attributed this to their apparent enjoyment of living this way, remaining in "[...] their more dense condition of nastiness, in which they apparently delight to exist" (ibid.).

In June of 1870, the anti-Chinese movement had already been validated by the same arguments that demanded this type of inspection by the Board of Supervisors, and they were trying to find a way to banish the Chinese to outside the city limits. This case was brought about through a petition submitted by Thomas Mooney and Hugh Murray, the president and vice president of the Anti-Coolie Association (McClain 1994, 44). One month later, at a mass event organized by a shoemaker's association, Mooney gave an open hate speech, proclaiming that everyone needed to "[...] use those powers bestowed on you by the God of the universe to hurl from your midst this abominable clay-colored race, stained with every crime and abomination known to ancient or modern barbarianism" (ibid.).[79] Like many other members of 'anti-coolie' associations, he first argued that it was about choosing between free labor and slavery, to which the Chinese in California were supposedly subjected. This was followed by calls for the implementation of legislation to stop Chinese immigration both at the local and the federal level (ibid.).

79 As quoted in: *Chronicle*, July 8, 1870, p. 2, col. 3.

In the years that followed, legislation was passed that discriminated against Chinese residents and immigrants at the state level (such as the 1873 law that seriously affected the vital sector of laundrymen in California), and at the national level (like the Page Law against the immigration of Chinese prostitutes in 1875, see more below).

If the working sector was one of the most active in the promotion of excluding Chinese from the country, the constant harassment and persecution of them was especially propagated by the Workingmen's Party of California, founded by the Irish immigrant Dennis Kearney in 1877. With the slogan "The Chinese Must Go!" (Lee 2003, 26) they loudly advocated for the exclusion of Chinese from California, particularly the workers. In addition to calling for plundering and expulsing the Chinese, their platform also propagated the confiscation of latifundia, therefore creating an opposition among the European American elite. In November of 1878, one-third of the assemblymen who participated in the constitutional assembly in the capital city of Sacramento were delegates of this radical party. Therefore, they played an important role in the design and consequent adoption of new articles in the new state constitution that replaced the 1849 state constitution. Approved in 1879 and taking effect in 1880, it was the most discriminatory constitution against Chinese in the entire nation (McClain 1994, 80-83). Article XIX entitled "CHINESE" prohibited Chinese from working in corporations and public works, unless they were prisoners. It further declared:

> The presence of foreigners ineligible to become citizens of the United States is declared to be dangerous to the well-being of the State, and the Legislature shall discourage their immigration by all the means within its power. (*Constitution of the State of California* 1879 Art. XIX, §4)

Because the Chinese, unlike European and African Americans, were not allowed to become citizens, this paragraph would serve as the basis to halt Chinese immigration to the state starting in 1880. Furthermore, that same year, the Treaty of Burlingame was annulled, which can be interpreted as a prelude to the coming era of exclusion.

Looking at other parts of California, the economic decline and a rise in the nationalist and racist workers movement did not fully explain the violence that was unleashed on the Chinese, as Zesch (2008) suggests in his analysis of the 1871 lynching of 18 Chinese residents in Los Angeles. According to this study, the 178 Chinese that were living in Los Angeles at the time were only about 3% of the population of 5,728 and they did not compete for the same jobs as their European and Latin American peers (ibid., 109, 112). It concluded that, apart from a conflict among the members of the Chinese community, the biggest cause of the massacre seems to have been a mixture of pre-existing racist animosity, the opportunity of acting with impunity (on the part of the victimizers), and the complicity of the local elite. The residents of both European and Latin American decent had participated in the riots, but "[...] the subsequent indictments for murder 'were against poor Mexicans without influence, and a lone Irishman, a shoemaker'" (ibid., 144). Of the some 500 people that had persecuted and lynched the Chinese, only eight were convicted and sentenced to between two and six years in prison. Eventually, one year later, the sentences were overturned because "the original indictments against them failed to specify that anyone had actually been murdered" (ibid., 145). According to Elliott Barkan, in the communities where few Chinese lived, this type of anti-Chinese violence was not common: "[...] they were often spared the worst conflicts, especially if they operated businesses or made some efforts to acculturate or interact with non-Chinese" (Barkan 2007, 60).

This perspective can be problematic because it can implicate that the Chinese were mostly responsible for their own exclusion and discrimination. It must be emphasized that the many measures that were taken by a large part of the European American population against the Chinese from the start of their immigration surrounding the Gold Rush aimed at hindering the integration, settlement, marriage or nationalization of the Chinese, and therefore fostered the unequal treatment of them on racialized premises.

This contributed to the creation of Chinatowns through regulations that limited the areas within cities that Chinese immigrants were allowed to live, therefore effectively creating ghettos and 'parallel' societies around North America. According to Nayan Shah, the racialized cartography of these ghettos was created by the European American elites using knowledge about the "Chinese race" (2001, 18) that had been gained through "government investigations, newspaper reports, and travelogues" (ibid.). Shah also conclude that the logic of the European American authorities was marked by a self-referential process: "The idea of Chinatown as a self-contained and alien society in turn justified 'recurring rounds' of policing, investigation, and statistical surveys that 'scientifically' corroborated the racial classification." (ibid.). Huping Ling opined that "the majority of the white Americans were ignorant of the Chinese culture and their ignorance brought prejudices" (1998, 27). Once the Chinese community was defined as unequal and different to the European Americans by the European Americans themselves, conditions were created that allowed the practice of discrimination and violence against the Chinese with a considerable margin of impunity, and not only within this specific context, but in all of the US-American society.

On the other hand, the establishment of these ghettos contributed to the regulation of social and legal questions in the society. The lack of access to legal protection and other U.S. social services for a large part of the Chinese population fostered the strengthening of the Chinese associations. These served as the primary access points if problems and disputes arose, and provided a kind of protection and support for the Chinese residents. This was particularly seen in the city of San Francisco where the largest community of Chinese immigrants lived in the nineteenth century. In this respect, Thomas Chinn summarizes the presence of Chinese in San Francisco:

> In its early days, the Chinese community in San Francisco tended to be very self-contained. Widespread discrimination, differences in language and culture, and the threat of physical violence confined most Chinese to Chinatown for virtually all their activities. As a re-

> sult, the Chinese usually took care of their own. Instead of seeking help from the American social services and charities, a Chinese person in need of assistance would turn to his or her family or district association. Similarly, disputes were usually handled by a district association or by the Chinese Six Companies rather than by the American court system; and the tongs, rather than the police department, often provided protection. (Chinn 1989, 2)

Here there are three basic elements of the self-organized system of the Chinese society: mutual aid at the familiar and neighborhood level, and also at the level of confederations of the most powerful merchant associations in Chinatown. Depending on the seriousness of the individual case of social need or a legal problem the problem was raised from the head of a family (or if there was no family, which was the case for thousands of young men who were alone, their native-place associations) up to the highest level of the Six Companies. With the support came obligations, and in the case that someone did not fulfill them, the same gradual process applied to the resolution of conflicts. Chinn uses the word 'tongs' to refer to the secret societies from which some had formed thug squads that served their own interests as well as the security interests of the merchant class (Lyman 1964).

If we consider the fact that in the early decades of the second half of the nineteenth century the Chinese could not testify against European Americans in the court of law, that they could not participate as citizens nor were they allowed to represent a liability to the state it is understandable that, against the background of constant threats they had no other option than to turn to the established institutions in Chinatown, for better or for worse. An exception to these destructive dynamics was the state of Idaho. In 1870, more than a third of the population was Chinese, and they represented more than 60% of the miners. However, while the anti-Chinese sentiment proliferated in California, Idaho was "one of [the] few havens" (Barkan 2007, 60) for Chinese in the United States.

In the case of Chinese women, they suffered discrimination from three sides: above all, they were limited in their wish to emigrate to the United States by their families (both consanguine and in-laws) in China, by the patriarchal feudal system, as well as by the lack of economic solvency of their husbands who had already emigrated. As soon as they arrived, they again had to conform to the prevailing rules within the Chinatowns, which were also dominated by the local patriarchal elite. Furthermore, their immigration as well as their presence in the United States were extremely difficult because of the anti-Chinese sentiment that were to culminate in the laws against Chinese immigration in the 1870s (Ling 1998, 26-27). In fact, Sucheng Chan argues that the first law to exclude the Chinese was not directed toward workers, but against women who were suspected of having immigrated to work as prostitutes (1991a, 95). Regardless of some decisions in favor of the immigration of women as men's equals, the 1875 federal "Act Supplementary to the Acts in Relation to Immigration" was finally passed, which came to be known as the Page Law. Chan indicates that this law indiscriminately served to exclude the immigration of Chinese women and that its greatest impact was not felt by women working as prostitutes, but by all the other Chinese women (1991a, 109).

George Peffer adds that the actions of the United States consuls in Hong Kong showed that "[...] American prejudices against the Chinese transformed the Page Law into a more general restriction of Chinese female immigration" (1986, 42). In fact, this law cemented the inequality of the number of each gender among the Chinese immigrants beyond the most extreme of all the residents in the United States until the middle of the twentieth century. Furthermore, the mechanisms of exclusion this established would soon reach all of the Chinese immigrants and residents with the law of exclusion of 1882.

5. Inter-American Entanglements: Spreading Xenophobia?

This chapter will concentrate on the inter-American dimension from the late nineteenth century through the first decades of the twentieth century, which was a period in US-American history that has been identified as the 'era of exclusion.'[80] A comparison of the regulations that affected the Chinese communities, particularly in the United States, Mexico, and Cuba, will aid in identifying the dynamics and degrees of exclusion and inclusion of these groups and aims at gaining a better perspective on the transnational entanglements that characterized these dynamics and the actors involved. A key question will be to which extent these processes can be interpreted as the spreading of xenophobia, and if they cannot be interpreted as such, would it be more accurate to perceive them as local, independent processes?

5.1. Transregional Exclusion: USA and Latin America

In her work on the exclusion of Chinese immigrants in the United States, historian Erika Lee found that "[i]mmigration law [...] emerges as a dynamic site where ideas about race, immigration, citizenship, and nation were recast. Chinese exclusion, in particular, reflected, produced, and reproduced struggles over the makeup and character of the nation itself" (2003, 7). We agree with her argument and we understand it in the sense that the dynamics of immigration across the oceans on both sides of the Americas created a space of transcultural Euro-Afro-Asian-indigenous entanglements in which the dominant group, being the immigrants from Northern and Central Europe, forcefully imposed themselves on the indigenous inhabitants as well as on other immigrant groups on the basis of their

80 For a recent and excellent overview of the literature about Asian exclusion in the United States, see Chang K. (2016).

supposed 'white' supremacy. Therefore, this space included conflict and ruptures and was defined not only by the ideas, but also by the actions of the immigrants who let themselves be led by these ideas. They thus created (or shaped, as Lee puts it) new imaginaries of co-existence and otherness, establishing the foundation of parameters of distinction and preference that have dominated US-American idiosyncrasies up until the present.[81]

Lee conceptualizes the exclusion of the Chinese as "an institution that produced and reinforced a system of racial hierarchy in immigration law, a process that both immigrants and immigration officials shaped, and a site of unequal power relations and resistance" (Lee 2003, 7). Here, she is mainly referring to the so-called 'era of exclusion' in the United States, which formally began with the first federal law of exclusion, the Chinese Exclusion Act of 1882 (which was extended and adapted in succession) and lasted until it was abrogated in 1943. It is thought (and the reading of Lee's book also suggests) that the phenomenon of exclusion went far beyond being an institution that merely regulated unequal and racialized relations between immigrants and the authorities: Free Chinese immigration opened up a new space to reformulate the concepts of citizenship, nation, belonging, and exclusion that, until the nineteenth century, had only been defined according to the mobility of Europeans to the Americas and the forced mobility (especially of Africans) that they controlled. With that, Chinese immigration, both free and forced (coolie trade), can be included in a broader discussion that defined the development of nation states in the Americas between the second half of the nineteenth century and the middle of the twentieth century. Therefore, this contribution maintains that the issue reflected in unequal negotiations of belonging represented in the entanglements of the Chinese and other American inhabitants not only pertains to and concerns the entire country of the United States, but all nations and societies of the Americas and beyond.

81 For links to the political landscape surrounding migration and the persistence of current prejudices, listen to "American immigration and xenophobia." Interview with Erika Lee. ABC Australia, 2018.

In order to validate this point, it is helpful to refer to two observations about Chinese immigration in the American hemisphere. One has already been mentioned in the introduction and was argued by Adam McKeown: The development of the immigration policies in the Americas were influenced by the practices and ideas developed by the United States and Canada in order to regulate Chinese immigration at the end of the nineteenth century and beginning of the twentieth century. These marked the beginning of the development of a system that regulates borders with respect to migration at the global level. Despite the great problems that entailed the institutionalization of a system to regulate national borders, at the end of the nineteenth century,

> [...] the enormous legal, political, and administrative effort put into enforcing these laws would gradually shift the momentum in favor of borders, thus establishing the basic principles and practices of border control as an integral part of modern, liberal polities. (McKeown 2008, 122-123)

With that, liberalism found its limits[82] in the individual right to freedom of movement that certain groups were denied of, mostly for racist and xenophobic reasons, although they were framed within a concern for maintaining "the social harmony necessary in a self-governed society" (ibid., 124), a fear that Thomas Jefferson had already harbored in 1782 with respect to the possibility of promoting the immigration of foreign workers.

The other argument, which ties in with the first, stems from a meticulous study by FitzGerald and Cook-Martín on migratory policies in the Americas from the end of the nineteenth century to the mid-twentieth century. From an inter-American perspective, they argue that the processes of building nation states and representative democracies brought with them the implementation of racist principles that shaped migration law, favoring the immigration of (ideally

82 This logic also governed the dynamics of extractivist production and trade, the liberation of which only made sense for the elite, who maintained control over production, the circulation of goods, and prices.

Protestant) 'whites' and discriminating against the rest. This diametrically clashed with the central ideas of Western liberalism:

> The classical liberalism of the mid-nineteenth century exalted the liberties of citizens and economic activity unhindered by the state. In its ideal form, liberalism meant freedom of movement, exchange, and political participation. A representative system of government was the means to foster these principles. Rights were inherent and equally applicable to autonomous moral individuals within nation-states. (FitzGerald and Cook-Martín 2014, 2)

FitzGerald and Cook-Martín did not limit their study to North America, but produced a piece of work that compared the migration politics in and between the United States, Canada, Cuba, Mexico, Brazil, and Argentina, and included references to other Latin American countries. With that, they show that there was a nexus between migration, liberalism, and ethnicity that allows for the identification of discriminatory politics of migration and citizenship politics in line with what has already been expounded upon here. Within this framework, it is particularly interesting that they emphasize the "racist ideology" (ibid., 15) as a means to legitimate "the differential distribution of resources and treatment by racial group" (ibid.). As they aptly assume, according to the Critical Race Theory, "while race is a historical construct rather than biological fact, it permeates social life" (ibid.). In the case presented here, it can be observed that, although migration regulations were not the same in every country in the Americas, ethnic ascriptions have influenced, and continue to influence, societies and their migratory policies, the development of which are often based on racist prejudices.

The following will compare the politics and practices in question in the United States, Cuba, and Mexico during the last third of the nineteenth century. As already stated, the United States were increasing their pressure on Chinese immigrants and the restrictive regulations were gradually being implemented (although not in a linear, continual manner) from the local and state to the federal levels, beginning geographically in the State of California and the mining regions of the Midwest. According to McKeown, these dynamics of exclusion were present in the entire Pacific Rim: "Beginning in the 1850s, white settlers around the Pacific worked to keep Chinese at the margins of their communities, if not entirely excluded" (McKeown 2008, 121).

In the United States, in a certain way, the Chinese Exclusion Act of 1882 formalized a legal discriminatory framework at the national level that in practice had already been applied at the local level and in various states for more than thirty years. However, it took on a different a quality: It was the first migratory law in the Americas in the late modern period that was directed at an ethnic group. While the Chinese who had already immigrated before the government started implementing diverse measures to make it impossible for them to carry on with their lives, there was now an effort to hinder the access of new Chinese immigrants. This law marked a turning point where the United States began transforming from being a country for (free) immigrants to a country that started selecting new immigrants on the basis of racist prejudices. According to Lee, this was to influence the guidelines for the entire development of immigration regulation in the United States:

> Beginning in 1882, the United States stopped being a nation of immigrants that welcomed foreigners without restrictions, borders, or gates. Instead, it became a new type of nation, a gatekeeping nation. For the first time in its history, the United States began to exert federal control over immigrants at its gates and within its borders, thereby setting standards, by race, class, and gender, for who was to be welcomed into the country. (Lee 2003, 6)

These dynamics of exclusion were not exclusive to the United States, but were reproduced in other Anglophone communities "around the Pacific [that] were enclosed behind an anti-Chinese barrier" (ibid.) until the mid-1880s. Similar to what had been happening in California, parts of the labor movement also advocated for excluding Chinese and other Asians, finally managing to take these claims to the federal level:

> In the late nineteenth century, organized labor and racist interests elected in British Columbia (BC) instigated what became a cross-class consensus on the restriction of Asians that they then effectively pushed through on the federal level. (FitzGerald and Cook-Martín 2014, 144)

As it has been shown in numerous studies,[83] in the United States the law of 1882, its extensions and later modifications initiated a true era of exclusion that would formally continue until its abrogation in 1943, but it actually lasted until the adoption of the Immigration and Nationality Act Amendments in 1965 (Chin 1996, 276). Since the 1990s, the United States has again been establishing racist migration policies. During the period of formal exclusion, the United States laws did not formally exclude educated or wealthy Chinese immigrants, among them primarily students and merchants, but they did in fact make it extremely difficult to legally move between China and the United States, including Chinese residents who wanted to visit China and those who were denied entry when they returned.

The laws were often interpreted as a carte blanche to exercise unbridled violence. This was the case in the brutal massacre of Chinese miners who were killed by European and American miners in Rock Springs, Wyoming, in 1885 because the Chinese did not join their labor protests.[84] As Bromley noted, it seems that the mass of people who attacked and killed the more than thirty Chinese miners and expulsed more than 500 more, along with ransacking and burning their homes to the ground, were fully aware of the crimes they were committing: "No one was drunk. It was a sober mob!" (Bromley 1886, 5).

---

83 See Ngai 2005, Lee 2003, and Chan 1991, among others.

84 For a contemporary and detailed account of the massacre see Bromley 1886.

5.2. Transpacific Cooperation between Asia and Latin America and Resistance in the Late Nineteenth Century

During that period, the Chinese immigrants abroad were relatively poorly protected under the Qing imperial government because "the Qing government did not officially recognize the right to emigrate and was itself besieged by foreign and domestic enemies" (Young 2014, 98). In fact, it was not until 1893 that the government revoked the ban on emigration, which, however, did not change emigrants' status as stateless with no guaranteed rights (ibid.). Nevertheless, there was an initiative in China to protect the workers who had gone to Latin America and the Caribbean as coolies, where their working conditions were similar to those of African slaves. The coolie trade in Cuba was abolished in 1874 after a visit and exhaustive investigation by the Chinese Commission to Cuba, which included Chinese and foreign experts, who highlighted the exploitation and maltreatment of the Chinese coolies in this Spanish colony (Ng 2014, 60 and passim).

That same year, the inhumane coolie trade was abolished in Peru when representatives of the country signed the Treaty of Friendship, Commerce and Navigation in Tianjin (China). This established commercial and diplomatic relations between the two countries and opened Peru to free Chinese immigration, which was later strictly limited in 1909 (Lausent Herrera 2011, 70). In Cuba, thousands of Chinese participated in the Wars of Independence against Spain (Pérez de la Riva 2000, 265-274), therefore becoming part of the founding legend of the Cuban nation, which was consolidated in the 1920s and 1930s: "In Cuba, Chinese became 'model minorities' *avant la lettre* because of their participation in the late nineteenth-century independence wars" (Young 2014, 281).[85]

It can be maintained that the last fourth of the nineteenth century was marked by a process that differentiated between the English-speaking region of North America and parts of Latin America:

85 Italics in the original.

While the United States and Canada were adopting increasingly strict laws against Chinese immigration, the logic of which would later be applied to other immigrant groups, in colonial Cuba and other countries, this process would not set in until the twentieth century, despite persisting ideas and practices of whitening that had been firmly established among the 'white' elite in Cuba, Argentina, and other countries. In Mexico, however, for some time there was an openly favorable policy regarding Chinese immigration before it was converted into a diametrically opposing dynamic.

In Cuba and Peru, the coolie trade had been abolished, but the poor treatment of plantation workers persisted. This is shown in the discontent that led Chinese to rise up and participate in the Cuban Wars of Independence as *mambises* (independence fighters) to fight against Spanish colonial control between 1868 and 1898. In Peru, Diego Chou explained the reason that almost 2,000 Chinese coolies went over to the Chilean enemy's side during the Pacific War in 1879: "The treatment of the coolies by the Peruvian masters was so bad and prolonged that it was natural for these unhappy people to go against them in this type of situation" (Chou 2001, 211).[86] Nevertheless, in Cuba as well as in Peru, Panama, Jamaica, and other territories where coolie work was present, free Chinese communities were being established that were similar to the ones in California and British Columbia. Mostly forming in the cities (but in this case by both the old coolies and new immigrants), forms of coexistence were developing which, to a large extent, were based on mutual aid associations, although they were stratified under the control of Chinese chambers of commerce and their leaders (Wilson 2004, xi).

In Mexico, where there had been no coolie trade, Chinese immigration was driven by the country's program for economic modernization under Porfirio Díaz's military dictatorship, which began

86 These forms of resistance may have originated in the tradition of rural rebellions practiced by secret societies in Southern China, as shown in the rebellion of Pativilca in 1870 in which some 1,500 Chinese participated and of which around 300 were killed by the Peruvian military that was sent to help the landowners (Lausent Herrera 1994, 174-175).

in 1877 and ended at the beginning of the Mexican Revolution in 1911 (Chao Romero 2010, 25). This modernization had already started under the governments of Sebastián Lerdo de Tejada and Manuel González, and after the plan to attract European workers had failed, Mexico turned to China and Japan (Kunimoto 2009, 94-95). In 1875, the then Minister of Finance, Matías Romero, praised the benefits of the immigration of Chinese and other Asians to Mexico, emphasizing Transpacific relations:

> It seems to me that the only colonists who could establish themselves or work on our coasts are Asians, coming from climates similar to ours, primarily China. The great population of that vast empire, the fact that many of them are agriculturalists, the relatively low wages they earn, and the proximity of our coast to Asia mean that Chinese immigration would be the easiest and most convenient for both our coasts. (Quoted in *Revista Universal*, 1875, in Chao Romero 2010, 26)

However, despite multiple attempts, Mexico was not able to enter into a treaty with the imperial Qing government until the signing of the 1899 Treaty of Friendship, Commerce and Navigation (ibid., 27), which "also served to attract Chinese capital that was invested in mining, railroads and Mexican commerce" (León-Manríquez and Tzili Apango 2015, 117). One year early, a treaty of the same kind had been signed with Japan (Kunimoto 2009, 92), which, in contrast to the treaty with China, stipulated a bilateral relationship that ensured the same rights for both countries:

> In contrast to China, Japan appeared to be a more desirable ally with due to the Mexican government's intentions to diversify their international relations, reopen their contact with the Asia Pacific and promote regulated migration. It must not be forgotten that within the historic context, Mexico shared with Germany and Japan the status of "emerging power." (León-Manríquez and Tzili Apango 2015, 117)

5.3. Circular Migration and Transnational Networks

"Free and voluntary" (Chao Romero 2010, 27) migration between China and Mexico was established in both directions with the treaty of 1899. But even prior to that, the development of Chinese immigration in Mexico was closely interwoven with its neighbor to the North. Velázquez Morales noted that, mainly starting when the United States were closing their borders to new Chinese worker in 1882 and many Chinese residents were expulsed or turned away at the borders when they returned from voyages, the region bordering Mexico, particularly Baja California, "became a pole of attraction for Chinese who were trying to evade deportation [to China]" (Velázquez Morales 2002, 400).

Many of these migrants intended to return to the United States, leading to massive remigration, both between the Northern USA and Canada as well as between the South and East of the USA and Cuba, which also constituted a part of this irregular remigration scheme (Young 2014, 3, 99). Elliot Young's map shows that the main centers for irregular Chinese remigration to the United States during the era of exclusion were the Mexican ports of Ensenada, Guaymas, Mazatlán, Manzanillo, Salina Cruz, and Veracruz, La Habana in Cuba and the Canadian cities of Vancouver, Toronto, and Montreal; and in the British Caribbean it was Jamaica and Trinidad and Tobago (ibid., 3).

The most established intermediaries for the facilitation of immigrant labor were Chinese merchants living in San Francisco, California. They had already provided the workers for the transcontinental railway in the United States and sent temporary Chinese workers to the US-American states of Louisiana, Texas, and Alabama. And now, the Mexican government turned to these merchants to organize the recruitment of Chinese workers in Hong Kong and Shanghai, as well as their voyage to the Mexican ports (Chao Romero 2010, 27-28). Other Chinese were smuggled in from San Francisco and San Diego (Velázquez Morales 2002, 400). According to Chao Romero, this cooperation between economic interests of Mexican and Californian Chinese business men was organized similarly to Chinese immigration to California just decades before, playing a role of transcendental importance in the interwoven history of the Americas:

> [It] […] helped to lay the foundations for a broader Chinese "transnational commercial orbit" […]. [It] facilitated the licit, and illicit, movement of people and goods among China, Mexico, Cuba, and the United States, and it is what makes the case study of the Chinese in Mexico a unique example of Chinese transnationalism in the global Chinese diaspora during the late nineteenth and early twentieth centuries. (Chao Romero 2010, 28)

The development of these structures, which included illegal human trafficking, occurred at the same time as the establishment of an increasingly strict US-American regime of migration regulation. Apart from putting pressure on neighboring countries (Mexico and Canada) to support their system of exclusion based on ethnic discrimination, the United States used their imperialistic expansion, starting with the Spanish-American War of 1898, to spread their ideology of exclusion: In 1902, after the military occupation of Cuba and the Philippines, the United States decreed the application of the laws of exclusion of Chinese workers in these territories (Young 2014, 99; Alejandrino 2003).

5.4. Hegemonic Power and the Proliferation of Policies of Exclusion in the Americas

Already in 1898, after Hawaii was annexed, the United States prohibited Chinese immigration to these islands as well as the migration of the Chinese who already lived there to the continental US. The definition of those who were considered 'white', which excluded Asians, was continually being developed during this period: "From 1878 to 1909, eleven of twelve cases deciding racial prerequisites to naturalize ruled against their plaintiffs, thus declaring people from China, Japan, Burma, and Hawaii to be nonwhite" (FitzGerald and Cook-Martín 2014, 88). At the same time, Irish, Spanish, Italian, and European Jews were being more easily classified as 'white', because "white was understood to be 'European' rather than exclusively Anglo-Saxon" (ibid.), as Benjamin Franklin had been propagating in the mid-eighteenth century.

In 1902, the United States congress extended the exclusion of Chinese indefinitely (FitzGerald and Cook-Martín 2014, 95). Since the 1880s, both the measures the United States government took and the abolition of coolie trade had had an impact on the entire American hemisphere:

> Every country in the Americas passed some form of discriminatory immigration law after 1880 [...]. Chinese exclusions were the most common in the hemisphere. The other most commonly targeted groups were Japanese, Roma (*gitanos* in Spanish-speaking countries, *ciganos* in Brazil), blacks, and Middle Eastern immigrants [...]. (Cook-Martín and FitzGerald 2019, 55)[87]

Of the 22 countries in the Americas that the authors included in their study, 18 countries adopted laws against Chinese immigration in the 1930s (see the image ibid., 52). Regulation of immigration to the United Stated had an impact on other countries due to the sheer size of the country, its increasing power in the hemisphere, and its advanced position in transoceanic immigration. When the United States began excluding Chinese immigrants, the majority of the other countries in the Americas reacted immediately:

> [...] many governments imposed ethnic discrimination because they feared that U.S. bans on Chinese labor migration in the nineteenth century and restrictions of southern Europeans in the 1920s would redirect those groups to other ports. (Ibid., 58)

This was also the case with the Gentlemen's Agreement between the United States and Japan starting in 1907, which limited Japanese immigration, although only disparately: While Canada "almost immediately imposed restrictions modeled on the Gentleman's Agreement" (ibid.), Brazil and Japan agreed to facilitate Japanese immi-

87 Italics in the original.

gration in order to help foment the development of Brazilian agriculture.[88]

In order to regulate the detention and processing of immigrants from China and other countries, the immigration station on Angel Island was established in 1910 in California's San Francisco Bay. As we have seen, San Francisco had been a point of entry, which is why almost all immigrants to the United States entering from the Pacific passed through there. The Angel Island immigration station was then constructed similarly to the one that had already been established on Ellis Island in 1892. However, if Ellis Island was a place of immigrants' hopes and dreams, but also of rejection and deportation, on Angel Island, which ran until 1940, the primary objective was to stop transpacific immigration, not to facilitate it. Both islands were ports of entry for immigrants who wished to fulfill their dreams of liberty and prosperity; however, as Lee and Yung point out, Angel Island became a prison for many Chinese, for it was there that the anti-Chinese laws were carried out:

> The immigration station was inextricably tied to the "hundred kinds of oppressive laws" that discriminated against Chinese immigrants. [...] Chinese were subjected to longer examinations, interrogations, and detentions than other immigrants. (2010, 69-70)

As one of the detainees carved into one of the walls in Chinese characters: "Even if it is built of jade, it has turned into a cage."[89] This line is part of the poem depicted on the right side of this photograph.

---

88 From the perspective of the Japanese government, Brazil had not been a preferable destination for emigrants up until that point, but this changed due to the restrictive policies of the United States (Lesser 1999, 85). Between 1908 and 1941, more than 188,000 Japanese immigrated to Brazil (ibid, 91), making the Japanese community in Brazil the largest outside of Japan.

89 There is a translation on the corresponding plaque in the permanent exhibition of the immigration station on Angel Island (see also Lee and Yung 2010, 16). The reference was made to jade because of the green paint that dominated the building.

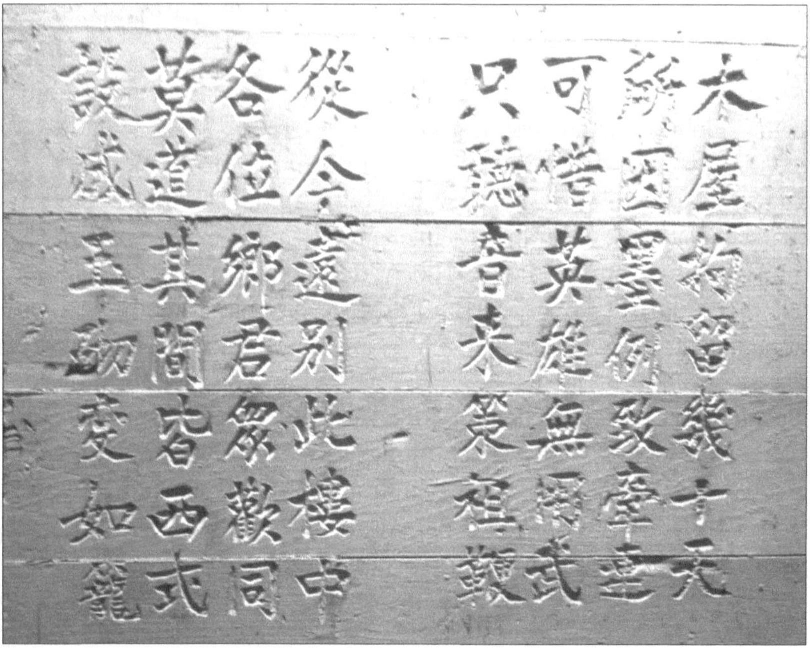

Restored inscription of two poems by an anonymous detainee at Angel Island Immigration Station, c. 1920s. Courtesy Albert Manke.

While the United States was able to establish its policies in the territories it occupied or controlled (such as Cuba and Hawaii) through its hegemonic control, this was not the case in other countries. As already mentioned, some countries, such as Mexico, wanted to attract Chinese immigrants despite the North American policies, which was to change with the new rise of nationalism during and after the Mexican Revolution. Others still looked to the United States when formulating their policies, but without pressure from the US government. This was the case with Colombia, where in 1887 the conservative government of President Rafael Núñez ordered the prohibition of "the importation of Chinese for any kind of work on Colombian territory" (quoted in Olaya 2018, paragraph 4).

Starting in the 1920s, an increase in the inter-American entanglements can be observed, and with this respect, the migration policies in the region were becoming increasingly similar. Countries began adopting standards of ethnoracist distinction that informed the development of these policies. This was facilitated and lead by the 'advances' and cooperation in the area of science, where transregional standards of ethnic classification were being established based on racist premises. During the First Pan American Conference on Eugenics and Homiculture in Havana in 1927, the experts "agreed that biologically selective immigration policy was a means to better national populations" (FitzGerald and Cook-Martín 2014, 59). In his study on the selection of the 'apt' immigrant in Colombia, Olaya noted that Domingo Ramos, then Secretary General of the conference and also the leading representative of the Cuban experts on eugenics, closely followed the example of the United States when drafting his proposals for migration policies. He was in constant contact with the US expert on eugenics, Charles Davenport, who had made a key contribution to the formulation of the Johnson-Reed Act of 1924 (Olaya 2018, paragraph 26).

According to Nancy Ordover, this act, also called The 1924 Origins Act, or The Immigration Act of 1924, established a system of quotas to limit immigration to the country on the basis of the 1890 census, which "was chosen in an effort to restrict further immigration by southern and eastern Europeans (particularly Jews, Slavs, Russians, and Italians) […]" (Ordover 2011, 301). This was due to the racist concepts of the time that had been established as the consensus among a large part of the 'white' elite in the Western hemisphere. Nationalism required citizens who adapted to the predominant concept of belonging, and this concept was profoundly racialized:

> Nationality and race were not divisible concepts and the national origins quota has largely been viewed as a deliberate and successful attempt to keep out those who were not Anglo Saxon or Nordic. [...] Western Hemisphere countries were not subject to a quota. Like previous enactments, it was a product of the desire to keep the United States as racially and culturally homogeneous as possible. It barred entry to those who were ineligible for naturalized citizenship (i.e.,

> who were not "white"), thus cutting off what remained of Asian immigration after nearly 50 years of anti-Asian exclusion legislations. (Ibid., 301-302)

Doris Provine affirms that the concept of 'race' and the development of immigration laws are interconnected, interpreting this interconnection as a result of the desire to separate people:

> The desire to separate people by race, and sometimes by religion, has often animated campaigns for exclusionary laws. These campaigns are sometimes successful, as in the adoption of what became known as the Chinese Exclusion laws in the late nineteenth century. (2013, 32)

Coming back to the 1927 conference in Havana, Domingo Ramos' ideas were largely inspired by the Johnson-Reed Act, which he "wanted to introduce in Cuba and in the rest of Latin America, trying to convince his contemporaries to recommend the implementation of this system of quotas to their respective governments" (Olaya 2018, paragraph 26). His ideas reflected those of eugenics and contemporary politicians, for they propagated a "betterment of the national genetic patrimony" (ibid.). However, the majority of the representatives from other Latin American countries did not agree to follow the guidelines of the United States, although they also were not "against racial selection of immigrants according to their place of origin" (ibid.). In other words, they all shared racist ideas, but they wanted to formulate their own migration laws. These laws were often based on concepts that had been developing in each country and not merely under the influence of a hegemonic power. An influencing factor was migration caused by epidemics or armed conflicts, such as the First World War, the Mexican Revolution, and the Russian Revolution. People fleeing from these and other scenarios

> [...] raised fears among the Latin American governments who perceived the immigrants, products of these conflicts, as human waste, biologically "inadequate" leftovers of the war. This perception was supported by the eugenic discourse based on hereditary principles

> that strived for a selection of the biologically apt man to "civilize" the continent. (Olaya 2018, paragraph 14)

The Mexican Revolution, however, not only produced 'undesirable' immigrants in other countries of the region, but it radically changed the social makeup of the country and redefined both the significance and the content of the Mexican national identity. As various studies have analyzed, there were two conjunctures in which the Chinese in Mexico were aggressively persecuted (Yankelevich 2004).[90] In 1911, the Chinese community that had flourished in the city of Torreón (in the state of Coahuila) was destroyed when Francisco Madero's troops killed more than 300 Chinese and five Japanese residents. This type of massacre occurred in other cases (such as the ones in the United States that have already been mentioned) in which they were "stripped, robbed and mutilated while their homes were being ransacked and burned" (quoted in González 2017, 19). After the hostility finally subsided, Chinese immigration to Mexico once again recovered and even grew during the 1920s (Chang 2017, 12). At the same time, anti-Chinese organizations were forming all over the country that were particularly strong in the northern states of Sonora and Sinaloa. (González 2017, 45).

In Sonora, activist and politician José Ángel Espinoza not only participated in the campaign to insult and expulse the Chinese in this province, but he wrote a meticulous analysis about it in order for it to serve as a type of manual for the expulsion of Chinese in the entire country. Catalina Velázquez Morales explains that the campaigns in Sonora and Baja California were organized by racist groups and individuals, "making use of a xenophobic, nationalist discourse [with which] they aimed to unite the population against groups of foreigners, in this case the Chinese, who maintained their hegemony with respect to trade" (2009, 43). In the case of Sonoran Espinoza, one can observe the type of nationalism that was being propagated. Putting forth the need to spread Mexican nationalist

90 Some of the first comprehensive studies on this were those of Hu-DeHart (1982) and Gómez Izquierdo (1988).

ideals just like in other parts of the world, such as France, Germany, Italy, and the United States (Espinoza 1932, 182), it was primarily oriented toward fascist movements in those countries. Besides his openly racist excesses against the Chinese, he combined nationalism with anti-Semitism:

> [...] it is only with the constant practice of this doctrine [of nationalism] that the nations can effectively be raised and gain their independence. We have seen more than once the troll face of these Jewish peddlers, with their filthy box they carry, that are dedicated to selling any and every kind of small hardware. (Ibid.)

Marked by the effects of the Great Depression of 1929 and the emergence of populist movements, the 1930s was a period in which nationalist tendencies were re-enforced in various Latin American countries, which was often accompanied by resentment toward foreigners. In Cuba, for example, the economic crisis particularly affected the Chinese who were self-employed or had small business; many of them returned to China. Those who stayed in Cuba were affected by the nationalist movements that, in 1934, brought the passing the Law of the Nationalization of Work. This required that 50% of industrial, trade, and agricultural jobs were to be given to Cuban citizens: "The Cuban nativist labor movement targeted all foreigners, but in particular Jamaicans and Haitians in agriculture and Spaniards, Jews, and Chinese in retail trade" (López 2013, 201). These laws went hand in hand with migration laws that excluded Asians, Jews, and other immigrant groups that were not awarded the same opportunities of participation and belonging that descendants of European immigrants were.

Chapter 5 Summary

This chapter has shown that, above all between the last decades of the nineteenth century through the first decades of the twentieth century, multiple forms of inter-American and transpacific entanglements can be identified with reference to Chinese immigration.

Laws and practices of exclusion on the part of the United States set the standards starting in 1882, and again with the introduction of a quota system in 1924. They created an important frame of reference for the entire inter-American hemisphere, although they were not adopted by all nations in the Americas. It can be observed that with the imperialistic interventionism of the United States (which approximately lasted from 1898 until the 1920s) exclusive regimes were established against Chinese and other Asians in the countries that were most dominated by US-American interference, which were Cuba, Puerto Rico, various Central American countries, and the Philippines in Asia. Even so, the strong Chinese immigration in these countries would come to establish the Chinese as an integral part of society despite continuously experiencing discrimination.

In other countries that were not as much a subject of US-American control, the development of an immigration regime was more autonomous and depended more on the respective country's national or local development. In Mexico, which received almost no Chinese immigration in the nineteenth century, the government incentivized Chinese immigration in the late nineteenth century despite the United States' efforts to hinder it. Furthermore, both Mexico and Cuba were affected by the era of exclusion in the US since it was during this time that circular migration patterns developed that led to the entanglement of the Chinese communities in these and other countries in the Americas as well as over the Pacific. The development of these networks was shaped by the agency of the Chinese associations in a transnational, transregional, and transpacific way.

Nevertheless, if we want to answer the question regarding whether or not there was a spread of xenophobia, we cannot be inclined to give a mere affirmative or negative answer. The US-American influence in the formulation and application of discriminatory regulations and practices against Chinese is undeniable. But by the same token, it has to be kept in mind the racist ideas that existed among the elite and parts of Latin American societies that also shaped policies of exclusion. Some of the congruencies and contradictions in the development of transnational migration regimes can be observed around the above mentioned First Pan American Conference on Eugenics and Homiculture in Havana in 1927. However, we conclude that the spread of xenophobia occurred in a multi-centered manner, depending on both each nation's internal development and the inter-American dynamics between the countries in the entire region.

Conclusions

This study has examined the exclusion and discrimination of free Chinese immigrants in the Americas from two perspectives: from the comparative perspective and the perspective of interconnections. Firstly, it analyzed two important conjunctures of exclusion during two very different phases: The free Chinese immigration to the Philippines during the Spanish colonial period, and free Chinese immigration to California, including references to Mexico, Cuba, Canada, and other countries in the Americas from the mid-nineteenth century through the early twentieth century.

With a particular focus on the community of Sangleyes in Manila, the first conjuncture shows that the xenophobic attitudes and practices of the Spanish conquistadores and colonizers of the period were present within a border space. This space, in contrast to the territories on the American continent, was characterized by Asian powers that the Spanish perceived as powerful enemies, being the Empires of China and Japan. At the same time, similar to the Caribbean, it constituted a space of conflict between the interests of other European (Portuguese and Dutch) powers who were competing for colonial and economic domination in Southeast Asia. The Chinese immigrants, most of who belonged to a network of merchants who were well-established in the coastal province of Fujian in Southeast China, saw an opportunity for themselves in both transpacific trade (Manila Galleon) and local retail. They became indispensable in both areas because the conquistadores and colonizers who had immigrated from Spain, and especially from New Spain, were not able to establish a competitive retail trade system. They also did not control the commercial routes in the South China Sea, and with that they were doubly dependent on the Sangleyes. However, besides using multiple methods of control, exploitation, and submission against the Chinese, when the Spanish saw themselves threatened or if they had the impression that their power over the colony was weakening, they used forms of physical violence, even carrying out massacres that nearly exterminated the Chinese community in Manila.

The response of the Chinese community to maltreatment was neither uniform nor constant: While the Sangley merchants often tried to maintain their position of privilege, acting as intermediaries between the Spaniards and the Chinese workers, the workers tended to react faster to the exploitation and maltreatment with rebellion. Furthermore, as we have seen, the Chinese community eventually recuperated from the massacres and later represented the most important mestizo group in the Philippines by marrying into the Filipino population. In its entirety, Chinese immigration to the Philippines constituted a key element in the development and functioning of the Spanish colony, and later in the founding of the Filipino nation. Without them, colonial society would not have worked. Therefore, the persecution on the part of the Spanish against the Chinese seems to have weakened the society instead of stabilizing it.

The second conjuncture emerged nearly three hundred years later, when a similar migratory phenomenon occurred in California, which the United States had taken from Mexico in 1848. Once again, an empire (in this case the United States) occupied territory in order to incorporate it under its dominion. This time, the territory had already been colonized by the Spanish and later went on to become a part of the United States of Mexico, although there were still thousands of indigenous people living there. Having been subjects under the Spanish, under the US domination the indigenous were practically exterminated. The Gold Rush began around the same time as the annexation of California by the United States, turning California into a desirable destination for immigrants from all over the world, among them thousands of immigrants from Southern China, especially from the Guangdong (Canton) province.

While the Spanish took Mexican silver to the Philippines in the sixteenth century, it was now the gold mines in Western North America that attracted Chinese immigration. After the heyday of the gold claims had passed (and also parallel to this), Chinese immigrants began working other jobs, especially in trade and as laundrymen, besides working in the construction of the railway. Both processes of interaction between Europeans and Chinese presented here are similar in the sense that the Europeans (Spanish and Anglo-Americans, respectively) felt they owned the territory they conquered and colonized, and they refused to let immigrants dispute their control. In the case of California, where there were immigrants from many other parts of the world besides China, this refusal was directed especially at Chinese immigrants, Chinese Americans, and other Asians that the European Americans considered to be ethnically and culturally inferior, which was the basis of their discrimination against them, hindering their citizenship, and fueling their intents to expulse them.

Although the patterns of exclusion are similar in the Filipino and Californian and inter-American cases, there are, of course, evident differences that are due to both the temporal and territorial distances as well as the social, political, and economic differences between the two cases. In order to connect both periods, we have kept in mind the *longue durée* perspective according to Fernand Braudel that allows for comparisons within a broader temporal framework, which in this case are linked by the European expansion in the Americas and Asia.

The third chapter of this study introduces the second perspective of the interconnected inter-American history and also seeks to serve as a link between the early modern period and the late modern period (also by being between the second and fourth chapter). Departing from the transition from forced migration to free migration, it shows how, in the case of the Chinese migrants (and those from different parts of Asia), this transition was codified by characteristics of ethnicity and belonging that demonstrate a high degree of inequality with 'white' immigrants (who came to be equated with Europeans). This was due to a combination of power, racialized adscription, social class, and gender, which generated conjunctures of discrimination and exclusion on the grounds of ethnic adscription and xenophobic prejudices.

The fifth chapter focused on making the inter-American and transpacific interconnections more visible. The point of departure was the question of whether or not the US-American hegemony (which particularly began with the ascent of the United States to its position of the greatest power in the American hemisphere in 1898) meant the configuration of the inter-American cooperation regarding migratory issues according to the US-American model. Or, more specifically, whether the discriminatory politics and practices around Chinese immigration were enforced through United States' pressure on other countries in the Americas. We have seen that there is no easy answer to this. If the US-American hegemony was evident in the countries that were directly affected by their imperialist and economic interests (such as Cuba, Puerto Rico, and various other Central American countries), it wasn't as unilineal in the case of other countries. It can rather be confirmed that each country protected their own interests and had their own limitations; this finding is in line with the research on US-American influence in Latin America starting in 1898.

Although the influence of the US-American model is apparent, it is evident that it was not the only model of immigration regulation that existed, as clearly reflected in the politics of 'whitening' that were carried out in Cuba, Brazil, Argentina, and in other countries (even since colonial times in some cases). Although there existed a confluence of exclusive and racist policies at the inter-American level, especially as a result of the closer Pan-American cooperation following the First World War, the United States was not the only country propagating them. These policies and practices were also not simply applied through the adoption of an established inter-American model in the entire region; they were rather influenced by the national, regional, and local development of and within each country, as with the case of the persecution and exclusion of Chinese immigrants and residents around the period of the Mexican Revolution. This revolution in turn served as a trans-regional model for the development of ideas, practices, and policies in Latin America, but not with regard to the regulation of the immigration of Asians.

Transpacific negotiations of bilateral and trans-regional agreements that also regulated migration between Asia and various other countries in the Americas are in turn related to the inter-American interconnections. At the end of the nineteenth century and beginning of the twentieth century, agreements and treaties between China and/or Japan, on the one hand, and Cuba, Peru, Mexico, Brazil, and the United States (to name the most central actors) on the other, tried to lessen the disastrous impact of the exploitation and exclusion of Asian migrants and residents or incentivize (as in the cases of Brazil and Mexico) Asian immigration. Another important element that goes hand in hand with these efforts to protect the immigrants is the agency of the actors in the Chinese communities in the Americas. As mentioned in chapter 5, these created their own networks in order to bypass exclusive policies and were able to establish alternatives routes and patterns of inter-American cooperation that were different from that of the national authorities. The mechanisms of mutual aid that originated from local community practices in China contributed to fostering resilience both in individuals as well as within the community and were necessary for the survival and development of these communities in order to confront discrimination. This has often been compared to the Jewish diaspora,[91] as indicated by Evelyn Hu-Dehart:

> This phenomenon in the Chinese diaspora […] has often been compared to the anti-Semitism experienced by the Jews in diaspora. In both cases, the resentment has something to do with the target group's ethnic distinctiveness, clannishness, foreignness and, simultaneously troubling and intriguing, their perceived excessive success in limited but distinct occupations, especially in shopkeeping or local commerce. (2010, 65)

91 For further comparisons between the Jewish and the Chinese diaspora, see the volume edited by Chirot and Reid (1997).

Finally, it can be concluded that the combination of both perspectives in this study, the comparative approach with intersecting, interconnected and connected histories offers a promising approach to the inter-American and transpacific interconnections from a diachronic perspective. The fusion of the concept of *histoire croisée* that was introduced by Werner and Zimmermann (2006 and prior) with the new currents of comparative history paves the way, as pointed out by Andreo (2017), to putting aside nationalist limitations, allowing notions of connectivity and flows that are adapted to cultural studies and the study of diasporas.

Both comparative elements as well as interconnection have been highlighted in the history of exclusion and discrimination of the Chinese in the Americas, with the innovative link between distant historical periods and emphasizing the change in the quality and frequency of the connected elements in the late modern period. Nevertheless, the objective of this study is no more than presenting a tentative approximation. The next step that I would like to take in my ongoing research will be to take a closer look at the multiple ways that the Chinese community in the Americas reacted to the dynamics of discrimination and exclusion. I am particularly interested in how, in some cases, the Chinese community was able to create safe spaces of coexistence and upward social mobility through their resilience, resistance, and adaptation, thus shaping the development of societies in the Americas despite the repeated setbacks they experienced.

Works Cited

Sources and Collections of Documents

1790 Naturalization Act, Sess. II, Chap. 3; 1 stat 103. 1st Congress. March 26, 1790. http://library.uwb.edu/Static/USimmigration/1%20 stat%20103.pdf.

1795 Naturalization Act, Sess. II, Chap. 19, 20; 1 stat 414. 3rd Congress. January 29, 1795. http://library.uwb.edu/Static/USimmigration/1%20stat%20414.pdf.

1798 Naturalization Act, Sess. II, Chap. 54; 1 stat 566. 5th Congress. June 17, 1798. http://library.uwb.edu/Static/USimmigration/1%20stat%20566.pdf.

"American immigration and xenophobia." Interview with Erika Lee. Broadcast: Thu 29 Nov 2018, 8:05pm. ABC Australia. https://www.abc.net.au/radionational/programs/bigideas/american-immigration-and-xenophobia/10550452.

Atlas, Laureano. 1761. "Aspecto Simbólico del Mundo Hispánico." Illustration. In *Theses Matemáticas de Cosmographia, Geographia y Hydrographia*, ed. Vicente de Memije. Manila: no ed. https://upload.wiki-media.org/wikipedia/commons/4/47/Laureano_atlas-aspecto_simbolico_del_mundo_hispanico.png.

[Burlingame Treaty 1868] U. S. Treaties, Etc. Andrew Johnson. *Additional Articles To The Treaty Between The United States of America And The Ta-Tsing Empire, Of June 18, 1858*. Concluded At Washington, July 28, 1868. Library of Congress, Rare Book and Special Collections Division, Printed Ephemera Collection, Portfolio 236, Folder 24. https://www.loc.gov/item/rbpe.23602400/.

California State Assembly, Office of the Chief Clerk: *Statutes and Amendments to the Codes 1850*. https://clerk.assembly.ca.gov/sites/clerk.assembly.ca.gov/files/archive/Statutes/1850/1850.pdf.

California State Assembly, Office of the Chief Clerk: *Statutes and Amendments to the Codes 1855*. https://clerk.assembly.ca.gov/sites/clerk.assembly.ca.gov/files/archive/Statutes/1855/1855.pdf.

California State Assembly, Office of the Chief Clerk: *Statutes and Amendments to the Codes 1862*. https://clerk.assembly.ca.gov/sites/clerk.assembly.ca.gov/files/archive/Statutes/1862/1862.pdf.

Constitution of the State of California 1879. State Office: J. D. Young, Supt. State Printing, Sacramento, 1880. https://archives.cdn.sos.ca.gov/collections/1879/archive/1879-constitution.pdf.

"East and West Shaking Hands at Laying Last Rail." 1869. Photograph by Andrew J. Russel. Oakland Museum of California. http://collections.museumca.org/?q=system/files/H69.459.2030_15-AROH_785_2.jpg.

Juicio del papel escrito en Manila, en veinte y cinco de marzo de mil seiscientos y setenta y siete, sobre que no se permitan de asiento los sangleyes en las Islas Filipinas, fols. 332–358, Archivo de la Provincia del Santísimo Rosario, series B, section Sangleyes, Documentos sueltos 1594-1730, in chronological order, doc. 30. Archive of the University of Santo Tomás, Manila.

Leland Stanford, 8th Governor, Republican, 1862–1863. Inaugural Address. Delivered January 10, 1862. http://governors.library.ca.gov/addresses/08-Stanford.html.

Murillo Velarde, Pedro, and Nicolás de La Cruz Bagay. 1734. *Carta hydrographica y chorographica de las Yslas Filipinas: dedicada al Rey Nuestro Señor por el Mariscal d. Campo D. Fernando Valdes Tamon Cavallo del Orden de Santiago de Govor. Y Capn.* [Manila, no ed.] [Map] Library of Congress. https://www.loc.gov/item/2013585226/.

"Report of Special Committee on the Condition of the Chinese Quarter, and the Chinese in San Francisco." 1885. Prepared by W. B. Farwell and John E. Kunkler. In *San Francisco Municipal Reports for the Fiscal Year 1884–85, Ending June 30, 1885.*

Published by the Order of the Board of Supervisors. San Francisco: W. M. Hinton, 164–214.

"Sangley in Boxer Codex." https://upload.wikimedia.org/wikipedia/commons/3/34/Sangley_in_Boxer_Codex.jpg.

Sino-Spanish codex (Boxer codex), ca. 1590. Boxer mss. II. Indiana University, Bloomington, Indiana. http://purl.dlib.indiana.edu/iudl/general/VAB8326.

Supreme Court of California. "THE PEOPLE, Respondent, v. GEORGE W. HALL, Appellant." Cal. 1854. 4 Cal. 399, 1854 WL 765 (Cal.). http://www.jonathantan.org/RLGN224/People_v_Hall.pdf.

"The Great Fear of the Period: That Uncle Sam may be swallowed by foreigners. The problem solved." San Francisco: White & Bauer [between 1860 and 1869]. Digital ID: pga 03047. http://hdl.loc.gov/loc.pnp/pga.03047. Library of Congress Prints and Photographs Division, Washington, D.C., 20540 USA.

U.S. Bureau of Census. 1975. *Historical Statistics of the United States: Colonial Times to 1970*. Bicentennial Edition. Washington, D.C.

[*U.S. Declaration of Independence*] *In Congress, July 4, 1776, a declaration by the representatives of the United States of America, in General Congress assembled*. Philadelphia: Printed by John Dunlap [1776]. https://www.loc.gov/item/2003576546.

Secondary Literature

Achiume, E. Tendayi. 2018. "Governing Xenophobia." *Vanderbilt Journal of Transnational Law* 51, no. 2 (March): 333–398.

———. 2014. "Beyond Prejudice: Structural Xenophobic Discrimination against Refugees." *Georgetown Journal of International Law* 45, no. 2: 323–381.

Albiez, Sarah, Philipp Kauppert, and Sophie Müller, eds. 2007. *China und Lateinamerika: Ein transpazifischer Brückenschlag*. Berlin: Wissenschaftlicher Verlag Berlin.

Alejandrino, Clark. 2003. *A History of the 1902 Chinese Exclusion Act: American Colonial Transmission and Deterioration of Filipino-Chinese Relations*. Manila: Kaisa Para Sa Kaunlaran.

Almaguer, Tomás. 1994. *Racial Fault Lines: The Historical Origins of White Supremacy in California*. Berkeley: University of California Press.

Amelina, Anna, and Thomas Faist. 2016. "De-naturalizing the National in Research Methodologies: Key Concepts of Transnational Studies in Migration." In Amelina, Faist, and Nergiz, 1–18.

Amelina, Anna, Thomas Faist, and Devrimsel D. Nergiz, eds. 2016. *Methodologies on the Move: The Transnational Turn in Empirical Migration Research*. London: Routledge. First issued in paperback.

Amelina, Anna, Devrimsel D. Nergiz, Thomas Faist, and Nina Glick Schiller, eds. 2012. *Beyond Methodological Nationalism: Research Methodologies for Cross-Border Studies*. New York: Routledge.

Amyot, Jacques. 1973. *The Manila Chinese: Familism in the Philippine Environment*. 2nd ed. Quezon City: Institute of Philippine Culture; Ateneo de Manila University.

Andreo, Igor Luis. 2017. "América Latina e as histórias transnacionais, conectadas e cruzadas: a comparação ainda é pertinente para o campo historiográfico?" *História: Debates e Tendências* 17, no. 1 (jan./jun.): 101–110.

Aoki, Keith. 2011. "The Yellow Pacific: Transnational Identities, Diasporic Racialization, and Myth(s) of the 'Asian Century'." *UC Davis Law Review* 44, no. 3 (February): 897–953.

Armentrout Ma, L. Eve. 1991. "Chinatown Organizations and the Anti-Chinese Movement, 1882–1914." In Chan, 147–169.

Asing, Norman. 1852. "To His Excellency Governor Bigler." In Yung, Chang, and Lai 2006, 9–12.

Bancroft, Hubert H. 1888. *California Inter Pocula*. San Francisco: The History Company.

Barkan, Elliott R. 2007. *From All Points: America's Immigrant West, 1870s–1952*. Bloomington: Indiana University Press.

Barrett, James R., and David Roediger. 2002. "How White People Became White." In *White Privilege: Essential Readings on the Other Side of Racism*, ed. Paula S. Rothenberg, 29–34. New York: Worth Publishers.

Barth, Gunther. 1964. *Bitter Strength: A History of the Chinese in the United States, 1850–1870*. Cambridge: Harvard University Press.

Bauböck, Rainer, and Thomas Faist, eds. 2010. *Diaspora and Transnationalism: Concepts, Theories and Methods*. Amsterdam: Amsterdam University Press.

Baxter, R. Scott. 2008. "The Response of California's Chinese Populations to the Anti-Chinese Movement." *Historical Archaeology* 42, no. 3 (The Archaeology of Chinese Immigrant and Chinese American Communities): 29–36.

Bell, David A., and Yair Mintzker, eds. 2018. *Rethinking the Age of Revolutions: France and the Birth of the Modern World*. Oxford: Oxford University Press.

Betts, Alexander, and Lena Kainz. 2017. "The History of Global Migration Governance." *RSC Working Paper Series* 122, Refugee Studies Centre, University of Oxford, Oxford. https://www.rsc.ox.ac.uk/publications/the-history-of-global-migration-governance.

Bjork, Katharine. 1998. "The Link that Kept the Philippines Spanish: Mexican Merchant Interests and the Manila Trade, 1571–1815." *Journal of World History* 9, no. 1: 25–50.

Blussé, Leonard. 1986. *Strange Company: Chinese Settlers, Mestizo Women and the Dutch in VOC Batavia*. Dordrecht: Foris.

———. 1981. "Batavia, 1619–1740: The Rise and Fall of a Chinese Colonial Town." *Journal of Southeast Asian Studies* 12, no. 1: 159–178. https://doi.org/10.1017/S0022463400005051.

Boatcă, Manuela. 2013. "Coloniality of Labor in the Global Periphery: Latin America and Eastern Europe in the World-System." *Review (Fernand Braudel Center)* 36, nos. 3–4 (Centers and Peripheries Revisited): 287–314.

Bonialian, Mariano A. 2012. *El Pacífico hispanoamericano: Política y comercio asiático en el Imperio Español (1680–1784) – La centralidad de lo marginal*. Mexico City: El Colegio de México.

———. 2014. *China en la América colonial: Bienes, mercados, comercio y cultura del consumo desde México hasta Buenos Aires*. Buenos Aires: Biblos.

Borao, José Eugenio. 1998. "The Massacre of 1603: Chinese Perception of the Spanish on the Philippines." *Itinerario* 22, no. 1: 22–40.

Bornstein, George. 2014. *Material Modernism: The Politics of the Page*. Cambridge: Cambridge University Press.

Bromley, Isaac H. 1886. *The Chinese Massacre at Rock Springs, Wyoming Territory, September 2, 1885*. Boston: Franklin Press.

Bruns, Claudia. 2017. "Anthropomorphe Europakarten im Übergang zur Frühen Neuzeit." *Zeitsprünge. Forschungen zur Frühen Neuzeit* 21, no. 1/2 (Der Körper des Kollektivs): 9–43.

———. 2013. "Rassismus" In *Gender@Wissen: Ein Handbuch der Gender-Theorien*, ed. Christina von Braun and Inge Stephan, 213–245. 3rd ed. Cologne: Böhlau UTB.

Cano Borrego, Pedro Damián. 2016. "Sangleyes: Los residentes chinos en las Filipinas españolas." *Revista de la Inquisición (intolerancia y derechos humanos)* 20: 213–242. https://dialnet.unirioja.es/descarga/articulo/5788783.pdf.

Carlin, Amanda. 2016. "The Courtroom as White Space: Racial Performance as Noncredibility." *UCLA Law Review* 63, no. 2: 449–484.

Carrillo, Rubén. 2017. *Las gentes del Mar Sangley*. Mexico City: Palabra de Clío. http://www.palabradeclio.com.mx/src_pdf/Las1542847956.pdf.

———. 2015. "Asians to New Spain: Asian Cultural and Migratory Flows in Mexico in the Early Stages of 'Globalization' (1565–1816)." PhD diss., Universitat Oberta de Catalunya. https://www.tesisenred.net/bitstream/handle/10803/380545/Tesi-Carrillo.pdf.

Chan, Sucheng, ed. 1991. *Entry Denied: Exclusion and the Chinese Community in America, 1882–1943*. Philadelphia: Temple University Press.

———. 1991a. "The Exclusion of Chinese Women, 1870–1943." In Chan, 94–146.

Chang, Gordon H. 2012. "China and the Pursuit of America's Destiny: Nineteenth-Century Imagining and Why Immigration Restriction Took So Long." *Journal of Asian American Studies* 15, no. 2 (June): 145–169.

Chang, Jason O. 2017. *Chino: Anti-Chinese Racism in Mexico, 1880–1940*. Champaign: University of Illinois Press.

———. 2016. "Towards a Hemispheric Asian American History." In Yoo and Azuma, 30–49.

Chang, Kornel S. 2016. "Reconsidering Asian Exclusion in the United States." In Yoo and Azuma, 154–170.

Chang, Robert S. 2012. "Centering the Immigrant in the Inter/National Imagination (Part III. Aoki, Rawls, and Immigration)." *Immigration and Nationality Law Review* 33, no. 2: 339–358.

Chang, Robert S., and Keith Aoki. 1998. "Centering the Immigrant in the Inter/National Imagination." *La Raza Law Journal* 10, no. 1: 309–362 [reprint from: *California Law Review* 85, no. 5 (1997): 1395–1447].

Chang-Rodríguez, Eugenio. 2015. *Diásporas chinas a las Américas*. Lima: Fondo Editorial de la Pontífica Universidad Católica del Perú.

Chao Romero, Robert. 2010. *The Chinese in Mexico, 1882–1940*. Tucson: University of Arizona Press.

Ch'en, Ching-Ho. 1968. *The Chinese Community in Sixteenth Century Philippines*. Tokyo: The Center for East Asian Cultural Studies.

Chen, Hsiang-shui. 1992. *Chinatown No More: Taiwan Immigrants in Contemporary New York*. Ithaca: Cornell University Press.

Chen, Yong. 1997. "The Internal Origins of Chinese Emigration to California Reconsidered." *Western Historical Quarterly* 28, no. 4 (Winter): 520–546.

Cheong, W. E. 1971. "The Decline of Manila as the Spanish Entrepôt in the Far East, 1785–1826: Its Impact on the Pattern of Southeast Asian Trade." *Journal of Southeast Asian Studies* 1971, no. 2: 142–158.

Chia, Lucille. 2006. "The Butcher, the Baker, and the Carpenter: Chinese Sojourners in the Spanish Philippines and their Impact on Southern Fujian (Sixteenth–Eighteenth centuries)." *Journal of the Economic and Social History of the Orient* 49, no. 4: 509–534.

Chin, Gabriel J. 2013. "A Chinaman's Chance in Court: Asian Pacific Americans and Racial Rules of Evidence." *UC Irvine Law Review* 3, no. 4: 965-990. https://www.law.uci.edu/lawreview/vol3/no4/Chin.pdf.

———. 1996: "The Civil Rights Revolution Comes to Immigration Law: A New Look at the Immigration and Nationality Act of

1965." *North Carolina Law Review* 75, no. 1 (November): 273–346.

Chinn, Thomas W. 1989. *Bridging the Pacific: San Francisco Chinatown and its People*. San Francisco: Chinese Historical Society of America.

Chirot, Daniel, and Anthony Reid, eds. 1997. *Essential Outsiders: Chinese and Jews in the Modern Transformation of Southeast Asia and Central Europe*. Seattle: University of Washington Press.

Chong, José Luis 2013. *Los sangleyes chinos en el comercio novohispano (1550–1800)*. Mexico City: Palabra de Clío.

Chou, Diego L. 2001. "Los chinos en la Guerra del Pacífico." *Revista de Historia de América* 129 (julio-diciembre): 197–224.

Christopher, Emma, Cassandra Pybus, and Marcus Rediker, eds. 2007. *Many Middle Passages: Forced Migration and the Making of the Modern World*. Berkeley: University of California Press.

Chu, Richard T. 2010. *Chinese and Chinese Mestizos of Manila*. Leiden: Brill.

Chust, Manuel 2015. "Sobre revoluciones en América Latina... si las hubo." In *Las revoluciones en el largo siglo XIX latinoamericano*, ed. Rogelio Altez and Manuel Chust Calero, 21–42. Madrid; Frankfurt am Main: Iberoamericana; Vervuert.

Cook-Martín, David, and David S. FitzGerald. 2019. "How Their Laws Affect our Laws: Mechanisms of Immigration Policy Diffusion in the Americas, 1790–2010." *Law & Society Review* 53, no. 1: 41–76.

Cyrill, Melissa. 2018. "Hong Kong-Zhuhai-Macau Bridge: Mainland Connectivity Key to Bay Area Ambitions." *China Briefing*. October 31, 2018. https://www.china-briefing.com/news/hong-kong-zhuhai-macau-bridge-mainland-connectivity-greater-bay-area-integration/.

Dal Lago, Enrico. 2009. "Second Slavery, Second Serfdom, and Beyond: The Atlantic Plantation System and the Eastern and Southern European Landed Estate System in Comparative Perspective, 1800–60." *Review (Fernand Braudel Center)* 32, no. 4: 391–420.

De Graaf, Lawrence B., Kevin Mulroy, and Quintard Taylor, eds. 2001. *Seeking El Dorado: African Americans in California*. Seattle: University of Washington Press.

De Sousa Pinto, Paulo J. 2013. "*Chinchéus* and *Sangleys*: Ten Remarks on the Chinese Presence in Melaka and Manila (16th–17th centuries)." *Review of Culture* 43: 59–69.

Descalzo Yuste, Eduardo. 2015. "La Compañía de Jesús en Filipinas (1581–1768): realidad y representación." PhD diss., Universitat Autónoma de Barcelona. https://www.tdx.cat/bitstream/handle/10803/323096/edy1de1.pdf.

DeWaard, Jack. 2015. "Beyond Group-threat: Temporal Dynamics of International Migration and Linkages to Anti-foreigner Sentiment." *Journal of Ethnic and Migration Studies* 41, no. 7: 1041–1067. http://dx.doi.org/10.1080/1369183X.2014.929940.

Dharmowijono, Widjajanti W. 2009. "Van koelies, klontongs en kapiteins: het beeld van de Chinezen in Indisch-Nederlands literair proza 1880–1950." PhD diss., Universiteit van Amsterdam. UvA-DARE, http://hdl.handle.net/11245/2.69536.

Díaz-Trechuelo, María Lourdes. 1962. "Grabadores filipinos del siglo XVIII." *Anuario de Estudios Americanos* XIX: 277–306. http://hdl.handle.net/10261/99630.

Dirlik, Arif. 1998. *What is in a rim? Critical perspectives on the Pacific region idea*. 2nd ed. Lanham: Rowman & Littlefield.

Elizalde, María Dolores, Josep M. Fradera, and Luis Alonso, eds. 2001. *Imperios y naciones en el Pacífico*. Vol. 1, *La formación de una colonia: Filipinas*. Madrid: Asociación Espanola de Estudios del Pacífico; CSIC.

Eltis, David. 2004. "Free and Coerced Migrations: The Atlantic in Global Perspective." *European Review* 12, no. 3: 313–328.

———, ed. 2002. *Coerced and Free Migration: Global Perspectives*. Stanford: Stanford University Press.

———. 2002a. "Introduction: Migration and Agency in Global History." In Eltis 2002, 1–31.

———. 2002b. "Free and Coerced Migrations from the Old World to the New." In Eltis 2002, 34–74.

Emmer, Pieter C. 2004. "Freie und unfreie Migrationen über den Atlantik und die Abschaffung des Sklavenhandels, 1550–1850." In *Über die trockene Grenze und über das offene Meer: Binneneuropäische und transatlantische Migration im 18. und 19. Jahrhundert*, ed. Mathias Beer and Dittmar Dahlmann, 289–302. Essen: Klartext.

Escoto, Salvador P. 1999. "Expulsion of the Chinese and Readmission to the Philippines, 1764–1779." *Philippine Studies* 47, no. 1: 48–76.

Espinoza, José A. 1932. *El ejemplo de Sonora*. Mexico City: [no publisher].

Faist, Thomas. 2018. *The Transnationalized Social Question: Migration and the Politics of Social Inequalities in the Twenty-First Century*. Oxford: Oxford University Press.

Firmin, Anténor. 1998. *De l'Égalité des Races Humaines: Anthropologie positive*. Paris: Librairie cotillon, F. Pighon, successeur, imprimeur-éditeur, Libraire du Conseil d'État et de la Société de Législation comparée, 1885, Nouvelle édition augmentée. Première édition.

FitzGerald, David S., and David Cook-Martín. 2014. *Culling the Masses: The Democratic Origins of Racist Immigration Policy in the Americas*. Cambridge: Harvard University Press.

Flynn, Dennis O., Arturo Giráldez, and James Sobredo, eds. 2001. *European Entry into the Pacific: Spain and the Acapulco-Manila galleons*. Aldershot: Variorum.

Flynn, Dennis O., Lionel Frost, and A. J. H. Latham, eds. 1999. *Pacific Centuries: Pacific and Pacific Rim History since the Sixteenth Century*. London: Routledge.

———. 1999a. "Introduction: Pacific Centuries Emerging." In Flynn, Frost, and Latham, 1–22.

Folch, Dolors. 2007. "Piratas y flotas de China según los testimonios castellanos del siglo XVI." In San Ginés Aguilar, 267–286.

García-Abásolo, Antonio. 2011. "Los chinos y el modelo colonial español en Filipinas." *Cuadernos de Historia Moderna* 10: 223–242. http://dx.doi.org/10.5209/rev_CHMO.2011.38678.

García de los Arcos, María Fernanda. 1999. "Grupos étnicos y Clases sociales en las Filipinas de finales del siglo XVIII." *Archipel* 57, no. 2 (L'horizon nousantarien. Mélanges en hommage à Denys Lombard, vol. II): 55–71. https://doi.org/10.3406/arch.1999.3515.

García Encina, Edgar A. 2016. *El libro bellamente ilustrado: el caso México. Historia a manera de galería*. PhD diss., Universidad Complutense de Madrid. https://eprints.ucm.es/40096/1/T38008.pdf.

García Gimeno, Jorge. 2017. "Tiempos de cambios: La transformación del sistema comercial español en el Pacífico durante la crisis del imperio." *Mundo Histórico* Año 2017, no. 1: 172–199.

Gassama, Ibrahim J., Robert S. Chang, and Keith Aoki. 1997. "Foreword: Citizenship and Its Discontents: Centering the Immigrant in the Inter/National Imagination (Part II)." *Oregon Law Review* 76, no. 2: 207–232.

Geggus, David P., ed. 2001. *The Impact of the Haitian Revolution in the Atlantic World*. Columbia: University of South Carolina Press.

Gil, Juan. 2011. *Los Chinos en Manila, siglos XVI y XVIII*, Lisboa: Centro Científico e Cultural de Macau.

Glick Schiller, Nina. 2012. "Transnationality, Migrants and Cities: A Comparative Approach." In Amelina, Nergiz, Faist, and Glick Schiller, 23–40.

Glick Schiller, Nina, and Noel B. Salazar. 2013. "Regimes of Mobility Across the Globe." *Journal of Ethnic and Migration Studies* 39, no. 2: 183–200.

Glossary on Migration. 2011. (International Migration Law No. 25) Ed. Richard Perruchoud and Jillyanne Redpath-Cross. 2nd ed. Geneva: International Organization for Migration. https://publications.iom.int/system/files/pdf/iml25_1.pdf.

Gómez, Alejandro E. 2006. "El síndrome de Saint-Domingue: Percepciones y sensibilidades de la Revolución Haitiana en el Gran Caribe (1791–1814)." *Caravelle* 86, no. 1 (L'Amérique latine et l'histoire des sensibilités): 125–155. https://doi.org/10.3406/carav.2006.2923.

Gómez Izquierdo, José J. 1988. "El movimiento antichino en México (1871–1934). Problemas del racismo y del nacionalismo durante la revolución mexicana." Diploma thesis, UNAM.

González, Fredy (2017): *Paisanos Chinos: Transpacific Politics among Chinese Immigrants in Mexico*. Oakland: University of California Press.

González-Ripoll, María Dolores, and Consuelo Naranjo Orovio, eds. 2004. *El Rumor de Haití en Cuba: Temor, Raza y Rebeldía, 1789–1844*. Madrid: CSIC.

Harris, Karen L. 2010. "Sugar and Gold: Indentured Indian and Chinese Labour in South Africa." *Journal of Social Sciences* 25, nos. 1–3: 147–158.

Herzog, Tamar. 2015. *Frontiers of Possession: Spain and Portugal in Europe and the Americas*. Cambridge: Harvard University Press.

Hirschman, Charles, Philip Kasinitz, and Josh DeWind, eds. 1999. *The Handbook of International Migration: The American Experience*. New York: Russel Sage Foundation.

Hitzbleck, Kerstin. 2015. "Einleitung: Transformationen des Fremden im Spätmittelalter und in der Frühen Neuzeit." In *Die Erweiterung des 'globalen' Raumes und die Wahrnehmung des Fremden vom Mittelalter bis zur Frühen Neuzeit / L'extension de l'espace 'global' et la perception de l'Autre du Moyen Age jusqu'à l'époque moderne*, ed. Kerstin Hitzbleck and Thomas Schwitter, 5–31. (*Itinera: Beiheft zur Schweizerischen Zeitschrift für Geschichte*, vol. 38) Basel: Schwabe.

Hobsbawm, Eric J. 1995. *The Age of Revolution: Europe 1789–1848*. London: Abacus. Orig. pub. 1962.

Hoerder, Dirk. 2002. *Cultures in Contact: World Migrations in the Second Millennium*. Durham: Duke University Press.

Hu-Dehart, Evelyn. 2010. "Indispensable Enemy or Convenient Scapegoat? A Critical Examination of Sinophobia in Latin America and the Caribbean, 1870s to 1930s." In Look Lai and Tan, 65–102.

———. 2007. "La Trata Amarilla: The 'Yellow Trade' and the Middle Passage, 1847–1884." In Christopher, Pybus, and Rediker, 166–183.

———. 1982. "Racism and Anti-Chinese Persecution in Sonora, Mexico 1876–1932." *Amerasia* 9, no. 2: 1–28.

James, Cyril L. R. 1980. *The Black Jacobins: Toussaint l'Ouverture and the San Domingo Revolution*. London: Allison & Busby, new revised edition. Orig. pub. 1938.

Jung, Moon-Ho. 2006. *Coolies and Cane: Race, Labor, and Sugar in the Age of Emancipation*. Baltimore: Johns Hopkins University Press.

Kanazawa, Mark. 2005. "Immigration, Exclusion, and Taxation: Anti-Chinese Legislation in Gold Rush California." *The Journal of Economic History* 65, no. 3 (September): 779–805.

Kemasang, A. R. T. 1982. "The 1740 Massacre of Chinese in Java: Curtain Raiser for the Dutch Plantation Economy." *Bulletin of Concerned Asian Scholars* 14, no. 1 (January–March): 61–71.

Kossok, Manfred. 1985. "El ciclo de las revoluciones burguesas españolas en el siglo XIX: Problemas de investigación e interpretación a la luz del método comparativo." In *La Revolución Burguesa en España*, ed. Alberto Gil Novales, 11–32. Madrid: Universidad Complutense.

Kraus, George. 1969. "Chinese Laborers and the Construction of the Central Pacific." *Utah Historical Quarterly* 37, no. 1 (Winter) (commemorative issue "The Last Spike is Driven" ed. by the National Golden Spike Centennial Commission): 41–57.

Kriesi, Hanspeter. 2004. "Political Context and Opportunity." In *The Blackwell Companion to Social Movements*, ed. David A. Snow, Sarah Anne Soule, and Hanspeter Kriesi, 67–90. 2nd ed. Malden: Blackwell Publishers.

Kueh, Joshua Eng Sin. 2014. "The Manila Chinese. Community, Trade and Empire, c. 1570–c. 1770." PhD diss., Georgetown University, Washington. https://repository.library.georgetown.edu/bitstream/handle/10822/712443/Kueh_georgetown_0076D_12743.pdf.

Kuhn, Philip A. 2008. *Chinese Among Others: Emigration in Modern Times*. Lanham: Rowman & Littlefield.

Kumar Mishra, Amit. 2009. "Indian Indentured Labourers in Mauritius: Reassessing the 'New System of Slavery' vs Free Labour Debate." *Studies in History* 25, no. 2: 229–251. https://doi.org/10.1177/025764301002500203.

Kung, James Kai-Sing, and Chicheng Ma. 2014. "Autarky and the Rise and Fall of Piracy in Ming China." *The Journal of Eco-*

nomic History 74, no. 2 (June): 509–534. https://doi.org/10.1017/S0022050714000345.

Kunimoto, Iyo. 2009. "La negociación del Tratado de Amistad, Comercio y Navegación de 1888 y su significado histórico." *Revista Mexicana de Política Exterior* 86 (marzo–junio): 91–100.

Lai, Him Mark. 2004. *Becoming Chinese American: A History of Communities and Institutions*. Walnut Creek: AltaMira Press.

Lal, Brij V. 1996. "The Odyssey of Indenture: Fragmentation and Reconstitution in the Indian Diaspora." *Diaspora: A Journal of Transnational Studies* 5, no. 2 (Fall): 167–188. https://doi.org/10.1353/dsp.1996.0012.

Lau-Fong, Mak, and Him Mark Lai. 1992. "Occupational Structures of Chinese Immigrants in Early Malaya and North America." *Southeast Asian Journal of Social Science* 20, no. 1: 43-66.

Lausent Herrera, Isabelle. 2011. "The Chinatown in Peru and the Changing Peruvian Chinese Community(ies)." *Journal of Chinese Overseas* 7, no. 1 : 69–113. https://doi.org/10.1163/179325411X565416.

———. 1994. "Les Chinois du Pérou: une identité reconstruite." *Journal de la Société des Américanistes* 80: 169–183. https://doi.org/10.3406/jsa.1994.1530.

Laviña, Javier, and Michael Zeuske, eds. 2014. *The Second Slavery: Mass Slaveries and Modernity in the Americas and in the Atlantic*. Münster: LIT-Verlag.

Lee, Erika. 2003. *At America's Gates: Chinese Immigration During the Exclusion Era, 1882–1943*. Chapel Hill: University of North Carolina Press.

Lee, Erika, and Judy Yung. 2010. *Angel Island: Immigrant Gateway to America*. New York: Oxford University Press.

León-Manríquez, José Luis, and Eduardo Tzili Apango. 2015. "México y Asia Pacífico: proximidades y distancias de una dilatada relación / Mexico and Asia-Pacific: proximities and distances of a long relationship." *Revista CIDOB d'Afers Internacionals* 110 (Relaciones Interregionales: Transatlánticas, Transpacíficas y Trans Euroasiáticas) (Septiembre): 113–139.

Lesser, Jeffrey. 1999. *Negotiating National Identity: Immigrants, Minorities, and the Struggle for Ethnicity in Brazil*. Durham: Duke University Press.

Lew-Williams, Beth. 2018. *The Chinese Must Go: Violence, Exclusion, and the Making of the Alien in America*. Cambridge/London: Harvard University Press.

Lin, Renchuan. 1990. "Fukien's Private Sea Trade in the 16th and 17th Centuries." In *Development and Decline of Fukien Province in the 17th and 18th Centuries*, ed. Eduard B. Vermeer, 163–215. Leiden: Brill.

Ling, Huping. 1998. *Surviving the Gold Mountain: A History of Chinese American Women and Their Lives*. Albany: State University of New York Press.

Look Lai, Walton. 2010. "Introduction: The Chinese in Latin America and the Caribbean." In Look Lai and Tan, 1–3.

———. 2009. "Asian Diasporas and Tropical Migration in the Age of Empire: A Comparative Overview." *Journal of Chinese Overseas* 5, no. 1: 28–54.

———. 2002. "Asian contract and free migrations to the Americas." In Eltis (2002), 229–258.

Look Lai, Walton, and Chee-Beng Tan, eds. 2010. *The Chinese in Latin America and the Caribbean*. Leiden: Brill.

López, Kathleen. 2013. *Chinese Cubans: A Transnational History*. Chapel Hill: The University of North Carolina Press.

———. 2004. "'One Brings Another': The Formation of Early-Twentieth-Century Chinese Migrant Communities in Cuba." In Wilson, 93–127.

Lucassen, Jan, and Leo Lucassen. 2009. "The Mobility Transition Revisited, 1500–1900: What the Case of Europe Can Offer to Global History." *Journal of Global History* 4, no. 3: 347–377. https://doi.org/10.1017/S174002280999012X.

Lucassen, Jan, Leo Lucassen, and Patrick Manning. 2010. "Migration History: Multidisciplinary Approaches." In *Migration History in World History: Multidisciplinary Approaches*, ed. Jan Lucassen, Leo Lucassen, and Patrick Manning, 3–35. Leiden: Brill.

Lyman, Stanford M. 1964. "Chinese Secret Societies in the Occident: Notes and Suggestions for Research in the Sociology of Secrecy." *Canadian Review of Sociology & Anthropology* 1, no. 2: 79–102.

Machuca Chávez, Claudia P. 2009. "El alcalde de los chinos en la provincia de Colima durante el siglo xvii: Un sistema de representación en torno a un oficio." *Letras Históricas* 1 (Otoño–Invierno): 95–115.

Mallari, Francisco. 1989. "The Spanish Navy in the Philippines, 1589–1787." *Philippine Studies* 37, no. 4 (Fourth Quarter): 412–439.

Marques, Leonardo. 2016. "The Contraband Slave Trade of the Second Slavery." In Tomich, 173–198.

Marquiegui, Dedier N. 1994. "Migración en cadena, redes sociales y movilidad: Reflexiones a partir de los casos de los sorianos y albaneses de Luján (Buenos Aires, Argentina), 1889–1920." *Estudios Interdisciplinarios de América Latina y el Caribe* 5, no. 1. http://eial.tau.ac.il/index.php/eial/article/view/1230.

Martín, Juan L. 1939. *De dónde vinieron los chinos de Cuba: Los jaca, los joló, los puntí y los amoyanos en la vida cubana. Con un apéndice sobre las ideas morales de Cuba*. Havana: Atalaya.

Martínez, María-Elena. 2008. *Genealogical Fictions: Limpieza de Sangre, Religion, and Gender in Colonial Mexico*. Stanford: Stanford University Press.

Matsuda, Matt K. 2012. *Pacific Worlds: A History of Seas, Peoples, and Cultures*. Cambridge: Cambridge University Press.

McClain, Charles J. 1994. *In Search of Equality: The Chinese Struggle Against Discrimination in Nineteenth-Century America*. Berkeley: University of California Press.

McClain, Charles J., and Laurene Wu McClain 1991. "The Chinese Contribution to the Development of American Law." In Chan, 3–24.

McKeown, Adam. 2008. *Melancholy Order: Asian Migration and the Globalization of Borders*. New York: Columbia University Press.

———. 2004. "Global Migration, 1846–1940." *Journal of World History* 15, no. 2 (June): 155–189. https://doi.org/10.1353/jwh.2004.0026.

———. 2001. *Chinese Migrant Networks and Cultural Change: Peru, Chicago, Hawaii, 1900–1936*. Chicago: University of Chicago Press.

McLeman, Robert, Jeanette Schade, and Thomas Faist, eds. 2016. *Environmental Migration and Social Inequality*. Heidelberg: Springer.

Meagher, Arnold J. 2008. *The Coolie Trade: The Traffic in Chinese Laborers to Latin America 1847–1874*. Revised ed. [Bloomington]: Xlibris.

Meyers Konversations-Lexikon: Eine Enzyklopädie des allgemeinen Wissens. 1890. Vol. 9, *Irideen-Königsgrün*. 4th completely revised ed. Leipzig: Verlag des Bibliographischen Instituts. https://ia800201.us.archive.org/2/items/meyerskonversati09meye/meyerskonversati09meye.pdf.

Montes Romero-Camacho, Isabel. 2008. "El problema converso: Una aproximación historiográfica (1998–2008)." *Medievalismo* 18: 109–247. https://revistas.um.es/medievalismo/article/view/91661.

Morales Martínez, Alfredo J. 2016. "Cartografía y cartografía simbólica: Las 'Theses de Mathematicas, de Cosmographia e Hidrographia' de Vicente De Memije." *Varia Historia, Belo Horizonte* 32, no. 60 (set/dez): 669–696. http://dx.doi.org/10.1590/0104-87752016000300005.

Munford, Clarence J., and Michael Zeuske. 1988. "Black Slavery, Class Struggle, Fear and Revolution in St. Domingue and Cuba." *The Journal of Negro History* 73, no. 1 (Winter–Autumn): 12–32.

Mungello, David E. 2009. *The Great Encounter of China and the West, 1500–1800.* 3rd ed. Lanham: Rowman & Littlefield.

Munro, Martin, and Elizabeth Walcott-Hackshaw, eds. 2006. *Reinterpreting the Haitian Revolution and its Cultural Aftershocks.* Kingston: University of the West Indies Press.

Ng, Rudolph. 2014. "The Chinese Commission to Cuba (1874): Reexamining International Relations in the Nineteenth Century from a Transcultural Perspective." *The Journal of Transcultural Studies* 2: 39–62. https://doi.org/10.11588/ts.2014.2.13009.

Ngai, Mae M. 2005. *Impossible Subjects: Illegal Aliens and the Making of Modern America.* 4th print. 1st paperback print. Princeton: Princeton University Press.

Olaya, Iván. 2018. "La selección del inmigrante 'apto': leyes migratorias de inclusión y exclusión en Colombia (1920–1937)." *Nuevo Mundo / Mundos Nuevos* (online) (Questions du temps présent). Published December 10, 2018. https://doi.org/10.4000/nuevomundo.73878.

Ollé, Manel. 2013. "El Imperio chino ante los ibéricos de Asia Oriental." In *Las vecindades de las Monarquías Ibéricas*, ed.

José J. Ruiz Ibáñez, 313–332. Madrid: Fondo de Cultura Económica.

———. 2013a. "La proyección de Fujian en Manila: Los sangleyes del Parián y el comercio de la nao de China." In *Un océano de seda y plata: El universo económico del Galeón de Manila*, ed. Salvador Bernabéu Albert, and Carlos Martínez Shaw, 155–178. Sevilla: CSIC.

———. 2009. "Manila in the Zheng Clan Maritime Networks." *Revista de Cultura / Review of Culture* 29: 90–104.

———. 2007. "La formación del Parián de Manila: La construcción de un equilibrio inestable." In San Ginés Aguilar, 27–49.

———. 2002. *La Empresa de China: De la Armada Invencible al Galeón de Manila*. Barcelona: Quaderns Crema.

Ordover, Nancy. 2011. "Johnson-Reed Act (the 1924 National Origins Act, or the Immigration Act of 1924)." In *Anti-Immigration in the United States: A Historical Encyclopedia*, ed. Kathleen R. Arnold, vol. 1, 301–302. Santa Barbara: Greenwood.

Oropeza Keresey, Déborah. 2011. "La esclavitud asiática en el virreinato de la Nueva España, 1565–1673." *Historia Mexicana* 6, no. 1 (julio–septiembre): 5–57.

———. 2007. *Los "indios chinos" en la Nueva España: la inmigración de la nao de China, 1565–1700.* PhD diss., El Colegio de México.

Ou, Hsin-yun. 2009. "Mark Twain's Racial Concepts in Relation to the Chinese." Paper presented at Zhong Shan University, Guangdong, China. Published by the National University of Kaohsiung. https://ir.nuk.edu.tw/bitstream/310360000Q/10766/2/2009%E4%B8%AD%E5%B1%B1%E6%9C%83%E8%AD%B0%E8%AB%96%E6%96%87Mark%20Twain%27s%20Racial%20Concepts.doc.

Ownby, David. 1993. "Chinese *Hui* and the Early Modern Social Order: Evidence from Eighteenth Century Southeast China." In *Secret Societies Reconsidered: Perspectives on the Social History of Modern South China and Southeast Asia*, ed. David Ownby and Mary Somers Heidhues, 34–67. Armonk: M. E. Sharpe.

Peffer, George A. 1986. "Forbidden Families: Emigration Experiences of Chinese Women under the Page Law, 1875–1882." *Journal of American Ethnic History* 6, no. 1 (Fall): 28–46.

Pérez de la Riva, Juan. 2000. *Los culíes chinos en Cuba (1847–1874): Contribución al estudio de la inmigración contratada en el Caribe*. Havana: Ciencias Sociales.

Phelan, John L. 2011. *The Hispanization of the Philippines: Spanish Aims and Filipino Responses, 1565–1700*. Madison: The University of Wisconsin Press. Orig. pub. 1959.

Portes, Alejandro. 1999. "Immigration Theory for a New Century: Some Problems and Opportunities." In Hirschman, Kasinitz, and DeWind, 21–33.

Pratt, Mary L. 2008. *Imperial Eyes: Travel Writing and Transculturation*. 2nd ed. London: Routledge.

Preen, Mark. 2019. "What is the Greater Bay Area Plan?" *China Briefing*, February 21. https://www.china-briefing.com/news/the-greater-bay-area-plan-china/.

Provine, Doris M. 2013. "Institutional Racism in Enforcing Immigration Law." *Norteamérica* 8 (Supplement): 31–53.

Ptak, Roderich, ed. 1987. *Portuguese Asia: Aspects in History and Economic History (Sixteenth and Seventeenth Centuries)*. Stuttgart: Franz Steiner.

Rahn Phillips, Carla. 2007. "The Organization of Oceanic Empires: The Iberian World in the Habsburg Period." In *Seascapes: Maritime Histories, Littoral Cultures, and Transoceanic Exchanges*, ed. Jerry H. Bentley, Kären Wigen, and Renate Bridenthal, 71–88. Honolulu: University of Hawai'i Press.

Rediker, Marcus, Cassandra Pybus, and Emma Christopher. 2007. "Introduction." In Christopher, Pybus and Rediker, 1–19.

Rodríguez Pastor, Humberto. 2005. "Abolición de la esclavitud en el Perú y su continuidad." *Investigaciones Sociales* 9, no. 15: 441–456. https://doi.org/10.15381/is.v9i15.7008.

Ruiz-Stovel, Guillermo. 2009. "Chinese Merchants, Silver Galleons, and Ethnic Violence in Spanish Manila, 1603–1686." *Análisis* 12, no. 36 (septiembre–diciembre): 47–63.

Russell-Wood, A. J. R. 1992. *The Portuguese Empire, 1415–1808: A World on the Move*. Baltimore: Johns Hopkins University Press.

Sales-Colín Kortajarena, Ostwald. 2016. "Sangleyes en Manila: Algunas percepciones de las autoridades capitalinas, 1603–1630." *México y la Cuenca del Pacífico* 5, no. 13: 89–113. http://www.scielo.org.mx/scielo.php?script=sci_arttext&pid=S2007-530820160 00100089&lng=es&tlng=es.

San Ginés Aguilar, Pedro, ed. 2007. *La Investigación sobre Asia Pacífico en España: Granada 2006*. (Colección Española de Investigación sobre Asia Pacífico, 1) Granada: Editorial Universidad de Granada. https://www.ugr.es/~feiap/ceiap1/ceiap/ceiap1.pdf.

Schmale, Wolfgang. 2004. "Europa, Braut der Fürsten: Politische Relevanz des Europamythos im 17. Jahrhundert." In *Europa im 17. Jahrhundert: Ein politischer Mythos und seine Bilder*, ed. Klaus Bussmann and Elke Anna Werner, 241–267. Stuttgart: Franz Steiner Verlag.

Schrecker, John. 2010. "'For the Equality of Men – For the Equality of Nations': Anson Burlingame and China's First Embassy to the United States, 1868." *Journal of American-East Asian Relations* 17, no. 1: 9–34.

Schurtz, William L. 1992. *El galeón de Manila*. Madrid: Ediciones de Cultura Hispánica. Orig. pub. *The Manila Galleon*, 1939.

Seijas, Tatiana. 2014. *Asian Slaves in Colonial Mexico: From Chinos to Indians*. New York: Cambridge University Press. https://doi.org/10.1017/CBO9781107477841.

———. 2008. *Transpacific Servitude: The Asian Slaves of Mexico, 1580–1700*. PhD diss., Yale University. UMI Microform 3342671. Ann Arbor: UMI Dissertation Publishing, ProQuest LLC [2009].

Seijas, Tatiana, and Pablo M. Sierra Silva. 2016. "The Persistence of the slave market in seventeenth-century Central Mexico." *Slavery & Abolition* 37, no. 2: 307–333. https://doi.org/10.1080/0144039X.2015.1121024.

Shah, Nayan. 2001. *Contagious Divides: Epidemics and Race in San Francisco's Chinatown*. Berkeley: University of California Press.

Sinn, Elizabeth. 2013. *Pacific Crossing: California Gold, Chinese Migration, and the Making of Hong Kong*. Hong Kong: Hong Kong University Press.

Slack Jr., Edward R. 2010. "Sinifying New Spain: Cathay's Influence on Colonial Mexico via the *Nao de China*." In Look Lai and Tan, 7–31.

Somers Heidhues, Mary. 2009. "1740 and the Chinese Massacre in Batavia: Some German Eyewitness Accounts." *Archipel* 77: 117–147. https://doi.org/10.3406/arch.2009.4127.

Speer, William. 1870. *The Oldest and the Newest Empire: China and the United States*. Hartford: S. S. Scranton; Philadelphia: Parmelee; San Francisco: H. H. Bancroft.

Stahler, Michael L. 1970. "William Speer: Champion of California's Chinese, 1852–1857." *Journal of Presbyterian History (1962–1985)* 48, no. 2 (Summer): 113–129.

Stern, Steve J., ed. 1987. *Resistance, Rebellion, and Consciousness in the Andean Peasant World: 18th to 20th Centuries*. Madison: University of Wisconsin Press.

Stinchcombe, Arthur L. 1994. "Class Conflict and Diplomacy: Haitian Isolation in the 19th-Century World System." *Sociological Perspectives* 37, no. 1 (Spring): 1–23.

Sugaya, Nariko. 2007. "Chinese Immigrants in the Spanish Philippines: Looking Through the Story of Hay Bing or Juan Imbin of Taal, Batangas." *愛媛大学法文学部論集. 人文学科編.* (Faculty of Law and Humanities of the University of Ehime, Japan) 23: 49–62. Published September 28. http://iyokan.lib.ehime-u.ac.jp/dspace/handle/iyokan/3920.

———. 1994. "The Expulsion of the Non-Christian Chinese in the Mid-18th Century Philippines: Its Relevance to the Rise of Chinese Mestizos." In *The Ethnic Chinese*, ed. Teresita Ang See and Bon Juan Go, 111–119. Manila: Kaisa Para Sa Kaunlaran.

T'ien, Ju-k'ang. 1989. "The Chinese Junk Trade: Merchants, Entrepreneurs, and Coolies 1600–1850." In *Maritime Aspects of Migration*, ed. Klaus Friedland, 381–396. Cologne: Böhlau.

Todorov, Tzvetan. 2010. *La conquista de América: El problema del otro*. Translated by Flora Botton Burlá. Madrid: Siglo XXI de España Editores.

Tomich, Dale W., ed. 2016. *The Politics of the Second Slavery*. Albany: State University of New York Press.

———. 2016a. "Civilizing America's Shore: British World-Economic Hegemony and the Abolition of the International Slave Trade (1814–1867)." In Tomich, 1–24.

Tomich, Dale, and Michael Zeuske. 2008. "Introduction: The Second Slavery. Mass Slavery, World-Economy, and Comparative Microhistories." *Review (Fernand Braudel Center)* 31, no. 2 (Special Issue *The Second Slavery: Mass Slavery, World-Economy, and Comparative Microhistories, Part I*): 91–100.

Tremml-Werner, Birgit. 2015. Spain*, China, and Japan in Manila, 1571–1644: Local Comparisons and Global Connections*. Amsterdam: Amsterdam University Press.

Trouillot, Michel-Ralph. 1995. *Silencing the Past: Power and the Production of History*. Boston: Beacon Press.

Twain, Mark. 2010. "The Treaty With China: Its Provisions Explained." *Journal of Transnational American Studies* 2, no. 1. https://escholarship.org/uc/item/2r87m203. Orig. pub. 1868.

Valdés Lakowsky, Vera. 1987. *De las minas al mar: Historia de la plata mexicana en Asia, 1565–1834*. Mexico City: Fondo de Cultura Económica.

———. 1983. "México y China: del *Galeón de Manila* al primer tratado de 1899." *Estudios de Historia Moderna y Contemporánea de México* 9: 9–19. http://www.historicas.unam.mx/moderna/ehmc/ehmc09/107.html.

Valladares, Rafael. 2001. *Castilla y Portugal en Asia: declive imperial y adaptación*. Leuven: Leuven University Press.

Vega Loyola, José J. 2017. "Asiáticos en Lima de inicios del siglo xvii." In *Relaciones intercoloniales: Nueva España y Filipinas*, ed. Jaime Olveda, 221–242. Zapopan: El Colegio de Jalisco.

Velázquez Morales, Catalina. 2009. "Xenofobia y racismo: Los comités antichinos en Sonora y Baja California, 1924–1936." *Meyibó* Nueva Época 1: 43–81.

Wang, Gungwu. 1990. "Merchants Without Empire: The Hokkien sojourning communities." In *The Rise of Merchant Empires: Long-distance Trade in the Early Modern World, 1350–1750*, ed. James D. Tracy, 402–408. Cambridge: Cambridge University Press.

Wang, L. Ling-Chi. 2008. "'The Oldest and the Newest Empires': U.S.-China Relations Today." *U.S.-China Media Brief*. http://www.uschinamediabrief.com/ee_empires.shtml.

Warren, James F. 2007. *The Sulu Zone, 1768–1898: The Dynamics of External Trade, Slavery, and Ethnicity in the Transformation of a Southeast Asian Maritime State*. 2nd ed. Singapur: NUS Press.

Werner, Michael, and Bénédicte Zimmermann. 2006. "Beyond Comparison: Histoire Croisée and the Challenge of Reflexivity." *History and Theory* 45: 30–50.

Wickberg, Edgar. 2001. *The Chinese Mestizo in Philippine History*. Manila: Kaisa Para Sa Kaunlaran.

———. 1997. "Anti-Sinicism and Chinese Identity Options in the Philippines." In Chirot and Reid, 153–183.

Wills Jr., John E. 2014. "A Very Long Early Modern? Asia and Its Oceans, 1000–1850." *Pacific Historical Review* 83, no. 2 (May) (Special Issue *Conversations on Transpacific History*, ed. Lon Kurashige, Madeline Hsu, and Yujin Yaguchi): 189–203.

Wilson, Andrew R., ed. 2004. *The Chinese in the Caribbean*. Princeton: Markus Wiener.

Windus, Astrid, and Eberhard Crailsheim, eds. 2013. *Image – Object – Performance: Mediality and Communication in Cultural Contact Zones of Colonial Latin America and the Philippines*. Münster: Waxmann.

Wong, Edlie L. 2015. *Racial Reconstruction: Black Inclusion, Chinese Exclusion, and the Fictions of Citizenship*. New York: New York University Press.

Yankelevich, Pablo. 2004. "Extranjeros indeseables en México (1911–1940): Una aproximación cuantitativa a la aplicación del artículo 33 constitucional." *Historia Mexicana* 53, no. 3: 693–744.

Yoo, David K., and Eiichiro Azuma, eds. 2016. *The Oxford Handbook of Asian American History*. Oxford: Oxford University Press.

Young, Elliott. 2014. *Alien Nation: Chinese Migration in the Americas From the Coolie Era Through World War II*. Chapel Hill: University of North Carolina Press.

Yu, Henry S. N. 2017. "Chinese Migrations." In *A Companion to Chinese History* (Wiley Blackwell Companions to World History), ed. Michael Szonyi, 343–359. Hoboken: John Wiley & Sons.

Yun, Lisa. 2008. *The Coolie Speaks: Chinese Indentured Laborers and African Slaves in Cuba*. Philadelphia: Temple University Press.

Yung, Judy, Gordon H. Chang, and Him Mark Lai, eds. 2006. *Chinese American Voices: From the Gold Rush to the Present*. Berkeley: University of California Press.

Yuste López, Carmen. 2007. *Emporios transpacíficos: Comerciantes mexicanos en Manila, 1710–1815*. Mexico City: UNAM.

Zapata-Barrero, Ricard. 2018. "Rejoinder: Multiculturalism and Interculturalism: Alongside But Separate." *Comparative Migration Studies* 6, no. 20. https://doi.org/10.1186/s40878-018-0090-6.

Zehr, Martin. 2010. "Mark Twain, 'The Treaty with China,' and the Chinese Connection." *Journal of Transnational American Studies* 2, no. 1, article 18. https://escholarship.org/uc/item/5t02n321.

Zesch, Scott. 2008. "Chinese Los Angeles in 1870–1871: The Makings of a Massacre." *Southern California Quarterly* 90, no. 2 (Summer): 109–158.

Zeuske, Michael. 2013. *Handbuch Geschichte der Sklaverei: Eine Globalgeschichte von den Anfängen bis zur Gegenwart*. Berlin: De Gruyter.

Zolberg, Aristide R. 1999. "Matters of State: Theorizing Immigration Policy." In Hirschman, Kasinitz, and DeWind, 71–93.

Zúñiga, Jean-Paul 1999. "La voix du sang: du métis à l'idée de métissage en Amérique espagnole." *Annales* 54, no. 2: 425–452.

INTER-AMERICAN STUDIES
Cultures – Societies – History

ESTUDIOS INTERAMERICANOS
Culturas – Sociedades – Historia

This interdisciplinary series examines national and transnational issues in the cultures, societies, and histories of the Americas. It creates a forum for a critical academic dialogue between North and South, promoting an inter-American paradigm that shifts the scholarly focus from methodological nationalism to the wider context of the Western Hemisphere.

Vol. 1
Raab, Josef, Sebastian Thies, and Daniela Noll-Opitz, eds. *Screening the Americas: Narration of Nation in Documentary Film / Proyectando las Américas: Narración de la nación en el cine documental*. 2011. 470 pp.

WVT Wissenschaftlicher Verlag Trier	ISBN 978-3-86821-331-7	€ 29,50
Bilingual Press / Editorial Bilingüe	ISBN 978-1-931010-83-2	$ 29.50

Vol. 2
Raussert, Wilfried, and Michelle Habell-Pallán, eds. *Cornbread and Cuchifritos: Ethnic Identity Politics, Transnationalization, and Transculturation in American Urban Popular Music*. 2011. 292 pp.

WVT Wissenschaftlicher Verlag Trier	ISBN 978-3-86821-265-5	€ 29,50
Bilingual Press / Editorial Bilingüe	ISBN 978- 1-931010-80-1	$ 29.50

Vol. 3
Butler, Martin, Jens Martin Gurr, and Olaf Kaltmeier, eds. *EthniCities: Metropolitan Cultures and Ethnic Identities in the Americas*. 2011. 268 pp.

WVT Wissenschaftlicher Verlag Trier	ISBN 978-3-86821-310-2	€ 29,50
Bilingual Press / Editorial Bilingüe	ISBN 978-1-931010-81-8	$ 29.50

Vol. 4
Gurr, Jens Martin, and Wilfried Raussert, eds. *Cityscapes in the Americas and Beyond: Representations of Urban Complexity in Literature and Film*. 2011. 300 pp.

WVT Wissenschaftlicher Verlag Trier	ISBN 978-3-86821-324-9	€ 29,50
Bilingual Press / Editorial Bilingüe	ISBN 978-1-931010-82-5	$ 29.50

Vol. 5

Kirschner, Luz Angélica, ed. *Expanding* Latinidad*: An Inter-American Perspective*. 2012. 292 pp.

WVT Wissenschaftlicher Verlag Trier	ISBN 978-3-86821-309-6	€ 29,50
Bilingual Press / Editorial Bilingüe	ISBN 978-1-931010-84-9	$ 29.50

Vol. 6

Raussert, Wilfried, and Graciela Martínez-Zalce, eds. *(Re)Discovering 'America': Road Movies and Other Travel Narratives in North America / (Re)Descubriendo 'América': Road movie y otras narrativas de viaje en América del Norte*. 2012. 252 pp.

WVT Wissenschaftlicher Verlag Trier	ISBN 978-3-86821-384-3	€ 29,50
Bilingual Press / Editorial Bilingüe	ISBN 978-1-931010-91-7	$ 29.50

Vol. 7

Kaltmeier, Olaf, ed. *Transnational Americas: Envisioning Inter-American Area Studies in Globalization Processes*. 2013. 278 pp.

WVT Wissenschaftlicher Verlag Trier	ISBN 978-3-86821-415-4	€ 29,50
Bilingual Press / Editorial Bilingüe	ISBN 978-1-931010-92-4	$ 29.50

Vol. 8

Raab, Josef, and Alexander Greiffenstern, eds. *Interculturalism in North America: Canada, the United States, Mexico, and Beyond*. 2013. 312 pp.

WVT Wissenschaftlicher Verlag Trier	ISBN 978-3-86821-460-4	€ 29,50
Bilingual Press / Editorial Bilingüe	ISBN 978-1-931010-99-3	$ 29.50

Vol. 9

Raab, Josef, ed. *New World Colors: Ethnicity, Belonging, and Difference in the Americas*. 2014. 418 pp.

WVT Wissenschaftlicher Verlag Trier	ISBN 978-3-86821-461-1	€ 29,50
Bilingual Press / Editorial Bilingüe	ISBN 978-1-939743-00-8	$ 39.50

Vol. 10

Roth, Julia. *Occidental Readings, Decolonial Practices: A Selection on Gender, Genre, and Coloniality in the Americas*. 2014. 284 pp.

WVT Wissenschaftlicher Verlag Trier	ISBN 978-3-86821-446-8	€ 26,50
Bilingual Press / Editorial Bilingüe	ISBN 978-1-939743-07-7	$ 32.50

Vol. 11

Thies, Sebastian, Gabriele Pisarz-Ramirez, and Luzelena Gutiérrez de Velasco, eds. *Of Fatherlands and Motherlands: Gender and Nation in the Americas / De Patrias y Matrias: Género y nación en las Américas*. 2015. 344 pp.

WVT Wissenschaftlicher Verlag Trier	ISBN 978-3-86821-528-1	€ 29,50
Bilingual Press / Editorial Bilingüe	ISBN 978-1-939743-08-4	$ 39.50

Vol. 12
Fuchs, Rebecca. *Caribbeanness as a Global Phenomenon: Junot Díaz, Edwidge Danticat, and Cristina García*. 2014. 298 pp.
WVT Wissenschaftlicher Verlag Trier ISBN 978-3-86821-533-5 € 26,50
Bilingual Press / Editorial Bilingüe ISBN 978-1-939743-09-1 $ 32.50

Vol. 13
Andres, Julia. *¡Cuéntame algo! – Chicana Narrative Beyond the Borderlands*. 2015. 202 pp.
WVT Wissenschaftlicher Verlag Trier ISBN 978-3-86821-569-4 € 25,00
Bilingual Press / Editorial Bilingüe ISBN 978-1-939743-11-4 $ 28.50

Vol. 14
Hertlein, Saskia. *Tales of Transformation: Emerging Adulthood, Migration, and Ethnicity in Contemporary American Literature*. 2014. 228 pp.
WVT Wissenschaftlicher Verlag Trier ISBN 978-3-86821-570-0 € 25,00
Bilingual Press / Editorial Bilingüe ISBN 978-1-939743-10-7 $ 31.50

Vol. 15
Raab, Josef, and Saskia Hertlein, eds. *Spaces – Communities – Discourses: Charting Identity and Belonging in the Americas*. 2016. 382 pp.
WVT Wissenschaftlicher Verlag Trier ISBN 978-3-86821-590-8 € 29,50
Bilingual Press / Editorial Bilingüe ISBN 978-1-939743-13-8 $ 39.50

Vol. 16
Mehring, Frank, ed. *The Mexico Diary: Winold Reiss between Vogue Mexico and Harlem Renaissance. An Illustrated Trilingual Edition with Commentary and Musical Interpretation* (includes color plates and audio CD). 2016. 244 pp.
WVT Wissenschaftlicher Verlag Trier ISBN 978-3-86821-594-6 € 29,50
Bilingual Press / Editorial Bilingüe ISBN 978-1-939743-14-5 $ 39.50

Vol. 17
Raussert, Wilfried, Brian Rozema, Yolanda Campos, and Marius Littschwager, eds. *Key Tropes in Inter-American Studies: Perspectives from the* forum for inter-american research (fiar). 2015. 374 pp.
WVT Wissenschaftlicher Verlag Trier ISBN 978-3-86821-627-1 € 29,50
Bilingual Press / Editorial Bilingüe ISBN 978-1-939743-16-9 $ 39.50

Vol. 19
Rehm, Lukas, Jochen Kemner, and Olaf Kaltmeier, eds. *Politics of Entanglement in the Americas: Connecting Transnational Flows and Local Perspectives*. 2017. 226 pp.
WVT Wissenschaftlicher Verlag Trier ISBN 978-3-86821-675-2 € 27,50
Bilingual Press / Editorial Bilingüe ISBN 978-1-939743-17-6 $ 32.50

Vol. 20
Britt Arredondo, Christopher. *Imperial Idiocy: A Reflection on Forced Displacement in the Americas*. 2017. 194 pp.

WVT Wissenschaftlicher Verlag Trier	ISBN 978-3-86821-706-3	€ 26,50
Bilingual Press / Editorial Bilingüe	ISBN 978-1-939743-20-6	$ 30.00

Vol. 21
Schemien, Alexia. *Of Virgins, Curanderas, and Wrestler Saints: Un/Doing Religion in Contemporary Mexican American Literature*. 2018. 218 pp.

WVT Wissenschaftlicher Verlag Trier	ISBN 978-3-86821-724-7	€ 27,50
Bilingual Press / Editorial Bilingüe	ISBN 978-1-939743-22-0	$ 32.50

Vol. 22
Fulger, Maria Diana. *The Cuban Post-Socialist Exotic: Contemporary U.S. American Travel Narratives about Cuba.* 2020. 266 pp.

WVT Wissenschaftlicher Verlag Trier	ISBN 978-3-86821-769-8	€ 32,50
Bilingual Press / Editorial Bilingüe	ISBN 978-1-939743-27-5	$ 36.00

Vol. 24
Kaltmeier, Olaf, Mirko Petersen, Wilfried Raussert, and Julia Roth, eds. *Cherishing the Past, Envisioning the Future. Entangled Practises of Heritage and Utopia in the Americas.* 2021. 176 pp.

WVT Wissenschaftlicher Verlag Trier	ISBN 978-3-86821-804-6	€ 23,50
UNO University of New Orleans Press	ISBN 978-1-60801-206-0	$ 27.50

Vol. 26
Raussert, Wilfried. *'What's Going On': How Music Shapes the Social.* 2021. 224 pp.

WVT Wissenschaftlicher Verlag Trier	ISBN 978-3-86821-811-4	€ 28,50
UNO University of New Orleans Press	ISBN 978-1-60801-199-5	$ 34.00

Vol. 27
Frank-Job, Barbara. *Immigration as a Process: Temporality Concepts in Blogs of Latin American Immigrants to Québec.* 2021. 138 pp.

WVT Wissenschaftlicher Verlag Trier	ISBN 978-3-86821-820-6	€ 20,00
UNO University of New Orleans Press	ISBN 978-1-60801-215-2	$ 24.00

Vol. 28
Roth, Julia. *Can Feminism Trump Populism? Right-Wing Trends and Intersectional Contestations in the Americas.* 2021. 166 pp.

WVT Wissenschaftlicher Verlag Trier	ISBN 978-3-86821-821-3	€ 23,00
UNO University of New Orleans Press	ISBN 978-1-60801-205-3	$ 26.00

Vol. 30
Buitrago Valencia, Clara. *Missionaries: Migrants or Expatriates? Guatemalan Pentecostal Leaders in Los Angeles.* 2021. 236 pp.

WVT Wissenschaftlicher Verlag Trier	ISBN 978-3-86821-818-3	€ 28,50
UNO University of New Orleans Press	ISBN 978-1-60801-210-7	$ 34.50

Vol. 31
Schwabe, Nicole. *De-Centering History Education: Creating Knowledge of Global Entanglements.* 2021. 92 pp.

WVT Wissenschaftlicher Verlag Trier	ISBN 978-3-86821-828-2	€ 18,00
UNO University of New Orleans Press	ISBN 978-1-60801-214-5	$ 21.00

Vol. 32
Manke, Albert. *Coping with Discrimination and Exclusion. Experiences of Free Chinese Migrants in the Americas in a Transregional and Diachronic Perspective.* 2021. 162 pp.

WVT Wissenschaftlicher Verlag Trier	ISBN 978-3-86821-829-9	€ 23,00
UNO University of New Orleans Press	ISBN 978-1-60801-207-7	$ 27.00

Vol. 33
Rohland, Eleonora. *Entangled Histories and the Environment? Socio-Environmental Transformations in the Caribbean, 1492-1800.* 2021. 92 pp.

WVT Wissenschaftlicher Verlag Trier	ISBN 978-3-86821-833-6	€ 18,00
UNO University of New Orleans Press	ISBN 978-1-60801-208-4	$ 21.00

Vol. 34
Kaltmeier, Olaf. *National Parks from North to South. An Entangled History of Conservation and Colonization in Argentina.* 2021. 210 pp.

WVT Wissenschaftlicher Verlag Trier	ISBN 978-3-86821-834-3	€ 27,50
UNO University of New Orleans Press	ISBN 978-1-60801-204-6	$ 32.50

Vol. 35
Raussert, Wilfried. *Off the Grid. Art Practices and Public Space.* 2021. 232 pp.

WVT Wissenschaftlicher Verlag Trier	ISBN 978-3-86821-835-0	€ 29,50
UNO University of New Orleans Press	ISBN 978-1-60801-213-8	$ 34.50

Vol. 36
Ravasio, Paola. *This Train Is Not Bound to Glory. A Study of Literary Trainscapes.* 2021. 114 pp.

WVT Wissenschaftlicher Verlag Trier	ISBN 978-3-86821-836-7	€ 18,00
UNO University of New Orleans Press	ISBN 978-1-60801-216-9	$ 21.00

Vol. 37

Schäfer, Heinrich Wilhelm. *Protestant 'Sects' and the Spirit of (Anti-)Imperialism. Religious Entanglements in the Americas.* 2021. 242 pp.

WVT Wissenschaftlicher Verlag Trier	ISBN 978-3-86821-855-9	€ 29,50
UNO University of New Orleans Press	ISBN 978-1-60801-209-1	$ 34.50